UNIX INTERNALS

INTERNALS

A SYSTEMS OPERATION HANDBOOK

MYRIL CLEMENT SHAW AND
SUSAN SOLTIS SHAW

TAB BOOKS Inc.

Blue Ridge Summit, PA

FIRST EDITION
SECOND PRINTING

Copyright © 1987 by Myril Clement Shaw and Susan Soltis Shaw.
Printed in the United States of America

Library of Congress Cataloging in Publication Data

Shaw, Myril Clement.
UNIX internals.

Bibliography: p.
Includes index.
1. UNIX (Computer operating system)   I. Shaw, Susan
Soltis.   II.Title.
QA76.76.063S5515   1987   005.4′3   87-18011
ISBN 0-8306-2951-3 (pbk.)

Questions regarding the content of this book
should be addressed to:

Reader Inquiry Branch
Editorial Department
TAB BOOKS Inc.
Blue Ridge Summit, PA 17294-0214

Contents

Acknowledgments

The authors wish to acknowledge the gracious assistance of the Santa Cruz Operation for providing XENIX System V. In addition, thanks are due to AT&T and Bell Labs for their support in the development of the UNIX operating system, without which this book could not exist. The concept of UNIX internals as an important topic was introduced to the authors in a course prepared and presented by instructors for AT&T Technologies. The authors greatly appreciate this introduction. Finally, although no conversations have ever taken place, the authors wish to acknowledge the wisdom and guidance of Maurice Bach whose knowledge and explanations of UNIX provided great support for this effort.

Introduction

It is possible to drive a car without knowing the inner workings of its engine. It is also possible to program a computer without fully understanding its operating system.

Simple knowledge of operating system commands and basic understanding of some of the less sophisticated options will suffice for many programmers, but certainly not all. Any programmer who needs to write efficient, sophisticated applications must have full operating system support. To accomplish their professional goals, they must understand their operating system environment fully.

The UNIX operating system environment is complex and elegant. It provides many clever solutions to difficult problems. It defines a multi-user environment suitable for the entire range of computer hardware from micros to the supercomputers.

This book offers an in-depth examination of how UNIX does its job: how it provides hardware and software services to programmers and users alike. That is the subject commonly called "UNIX internals."

This is not a book on programming. It is assumed that the reader possesses a working knowledge of C programming. Neither is this a book about how to use UNIX—the reader of this book may well be a UNIX user. The book provides a technically oriented description of how and why UNIX performs its various required functions—vital knowledge for excellent programming and for competent system management.

The material covered in this book will make any UNIX programmer who reads it a better UNIX programmer. It will help application developers to build their products around the strengths and weaknesses of the UNIX environment. Armed with the details provided in this book, programmers and programming managers will be prepared to use the best parts of UNIX and avoid its traps.

The UNIX operating system is more than simply an operating system. It is also more than an operating environment as is said so often. The UNIX operating system, by virtue of its design, is an example of how operating systems can be built. It handles problems and resolves complex situations in ways which are clever, creative and instructive.

The UNIX operating system is capable of handling files that contain up to 16 gigabytes of data. This is a remarkable feat for an operating system constructed for a PDP-7. Moreover, it can handle these 16 gigabytes without preallocating space or making demands on the location or placement of the data file. It can address every block in that 16 gigabytes with, in a worst case, no more than three disk accesses.

UNIX is probably not the best operating system ever designed. It is not necessarily the best at intelligently allocating processor time to the processes vying for that time—as they will in a time-sharing operating system. The mechanisms UNIX uses to store data on a disk probably result in considerable wasted space and relatively slow access times compared to some systems.

Despite the fact that in any single area UNIX may not be the very best—perhaps some of the algorithms could be improved—it does present an outstanding package. It is an excellent time-sharing system. Certainly some hardware environments into which UNIX has been forced do not show it at its best. Yes, it does tend to be disk intensive in systems with limited core. A system with a slow disk and limited core will make UNIX appear slow and cumbersome. Certainly the command structure associated with the UNIX shell is not the friendliest or easiest to learn. Nonetheless, UNIX has made its place.

At this time, the use of UNIX in business is expected to increase 200 percent over the next two years. The 80386 chip is anticipated to provide a microcomputer processor almost tailor-made to the UNIX operating system and its goals of fair time-sharing with sophisticated file handling. In addition to its already established role as an efficient and cost-effective choice for any small to medium multi-user environment, UNIX is beginning to make its impact felt in the single user multi-tasking market. UNIX use, which has been increasing at a slow but steady pace, should explode onto the data processing scene in an almost overwhelming way in the next two years.

This book is an effort to make that explosion somewhat less painful for those caught in its blast. The book serves three roles. First, it describes how the UNIX operating system works from the inside. Second, it illustrates the principles and problems involved in developing any multi-user, multi-tasking operating system. Third, it shows programmers those features of the UNIX operating system which directly affect the programming of applications—either positively or negatively.

A few books already on the market describe the internals of the UNIX operating system in a highly complex fashion. They expect, and in fact require, a fairly sophisticated computer science background in order to understand the blocks that put UNIX together. This book does not attempt to compete with those books: it is designed to supplement them. This book makes UNIX accessible to those who do not have a formal computer science, operating system background—for all those programmers and managers who must learn to deal with UNIX but who did not grow up with it. Of course, this explanation is provided at the cost of certain technical detail. Nevertheless, the fundamental principals of the operating and its internal design are clearly provided.

As algorithms for operating system development go, the approaches used in the UNIX operating system are excellent. All of the problems associated with operating system design are addressed. There are times when those of you excited by such things will cry out "That's really great!", or whatever it is you are wont to cry out at such times. The beauty of UNIX is that there are times when you will also cry out "But why do it that way?". The presentation of the algorithms and approaches to developing, designing and implementing a multi-tasking, multi-user operating system provide useful food for thought at worst and an excellent model if not an outright solution at best.

If an operating system cannot be understood and effectively used by the programmers working within its environment, then that operating system is a failure. This book shows programmers those areas and aspects of UNIX which directly affect the quality and efficiency of their programs. A programmer programming without a basic understanding of the operating system is like a race car driver driving with no understanding of high-efficiency engines. The basic skills may be there, but those subtleties which distinguish the good from the great will be missing. This book provides programmers with the tools of understanding needed for greatness.

This book is composed of 16 chapters in three parts. Like all good UNIX works, the first chapter is zero (all UNIX indexing begins at zero). The first part of the book, Chapters 0 through 5, focuses on the UNIX operating system as a whole and its program- and process-handling ability in general. The second part, Chapters 6 through 11, details the UNIX file system—from its user view to the details of the system calls that impact the file system. The final part, Chapters 12 through 15 concentrates on UNIX input and output. A brief summary of each chapter follows.

Chapter 0—UNIX Operating System Overview. This chapter outlines the topics to be covered throughout the book. It also provides a detailed description of the UNIX operating system environment.

Chapter 1—The Process Image. Programs are executed in the UNIX environment as processes. This chapter describes the actual structure of the process as it resides in memory before, during, and after execution. Also covered is the interface between the UNIX kernel and the process image.

Chapter 2—CPU Scheduling. All processes are given nearly equal amounts of time to run under UNIX. This chapter explains how processes are selected for execution, how they are deselected, and the criteria for process priority. The concepts of context switching (the switching between kernel and user processes) and how context switching impacts scheduling is also covered. Among the internal UNIX functions covered in this chapter are: switch( ), sleep( ), wakeup( ).

Chapter 3—UNIX Memory Management. As multiple processes are loaded into memory to be selectively executed, memory management becomes a crucial issue. This chapter covers primary versus secondary memory usage and the role of the primary swapper process. The actual sequences of events when one process is swapped out of memory and another swapped in is covered in this chapter. Also covered is the concept of the "sticky bit" for shared text processing.

Chapter 4—Inter-Process Communication. This chapter covers the techniques by which UNIX processes communicate between themselves. It discusses both the passing of information between processes and synchronization of processes. The major topics are messages, shared memory, pipes, signals, and semaphores.

Chapter 5—Process Creation. The fork( ) system call is the primary topic of this chapter. Except for the first three processes on a UNIX system, which are created at boot time, all UNIX processes are created by fork( ). The birth and death of processes is covered in Chapter 6.

Chapter 6—UNIX Files and Inodes. In this chapter, the four basic types of UNIX files and their structures are presented: regular files, directory files, device files, and named pipes. The role and usage of these files by the operating system is discussed. The function of inodes and their structure both on disk and in memory is also covered.

Chapter 7—The UNIX File System. The role and structure of the hierarchical UNIX file system is the topic of this chapter. Also covered here is the role of the superblock in the file system and the specific relationship between the file system and the physical disk device.

Chapter 8—The Superblock. Introduced in the preceding chapter, the superblock as it resides in memory is the topic of Chapter 8. Its structure and function are presented in detail.

Chapter 9—File and Inode Tables. This chapter describes how files and inodes are located and accessed by the UNIX operating system. It also describes how files can be enlarged and located in noncontiguous locations on the disk.

Chapter 10—Mounting File Systems. UNIX provides the unique capability of mountable file systems. The mount table, its role, and its structure are the topics of this chapter.

Chapter 11—System Calls to the File System. Access to the UNIX file system is provided through system calls. This chapter describes the operation of the system calls. The system calls covered include: stat( ), trap( ), namei( ), iget( ), iread( ), bread( ), getblk( ), iowait( ), brelse( ), stat1( ), iput( ), prele( ), plock( ), open( ), copen( ), access( ), falloc( ), creat( ), maknode( ), wdir( ), close( ), closef( ), pipe( ), openp( ), closep( ).

Chapter 12—Basic UNIX Input/Output. This chapter introduces I/O in the UNIX environment. It covers the interrupt-driver nature of UNIX I/O as well as I/O buffering. Also covered is the relationship between the kernel and the device drivers. System buffers and buffer caches for both block and character devices are reviewed.

Chapter 13—Terminal Input and Output. The techniques for processing keyboard and monitor input and output are covered in this chapter. The structure of the tty device file is presented and explained.

Chapter 14—UNIX Initialization and Termination. What happens at IPL or boot up time on a UNIX system? This chapter describes the processes which occur, which functions are initiated, and how the operating system gains control over the hardware environment.

Chapter 15—Miscellaneous UNIX Facilities. The final chapter covers those aspects of UNIX internal operation that have not fit into the other areas. Included in this chapter are the system time service, system accounting functions, the function of the system clock, and system errors and error handling.

This is not a book exclusively for programmers. Programmers who want more in-depth knowledge of the tools provided by UNIX should investigate *The UNIX V and XENIX System V Programmer's Toolchest.* If you want an in-depth and technically thorough view of UNIX internals you should also consult *The Design Of the UNIX Operating System,* by Maurice J. Bach. Beginners interested in the subjects covered by this book might want to consult *UNIX and XENIX Demystified.*

A noteworthy feature of this book is the "Points to Ponder" section included at the end of each chapter. This section provides a question or two for your thoughtful consideration. These are not simple questions with simple answers. They are intended to be thought provoking. All of the information needed to answer these questions might not be contained solely in this book—if these questions have satisfactory answers. By working through these questions, however, your knowledge of UNIX internals will be greatly enhanced.

This book is accessible and useful to all of the audiences described above. It makes the workings of UNIX understandable and at times enjoyable in a no-nonsense and clear way.

0
Overview

The UNIX operating system provides a rich programming environment for software developers. Students of UNIX find it "fun to work with" on an interface level, though both sophisticated and complex from the point of view of the techniques and approaches that comprise the environment. Study of the internals of the UNIX operating system reveals a complete and successful set of approaches to the creation of a multiprocessing operating system.

UNIX can be defined most simply as a timesharing operating system. It is designed to provide computing resources (more specifically computer processor resources) in a fair manner for a large community of users. This fair allocation of computer resources creates the illusion that each user has a complete computer system for private use, even though the truth may be that many people are actually sharing the computer and its processor at the same time. UNIX offers a time slice or what is sometimes called a *time quantum* approach to providing resources to each user. A complex and self-adjusting scheduling algorithm ensures that all users are treated fairly.

UNIX is more than a simple timesharing operating system—it is also a programming and processing environment. Although not strictly a part of the operating system kernel, UNIX provides a full set of program development and debugging tools. These tools aid significantly in the development of sophisticated programs and applications. The overall processing environment provided by UNIX also aids in the testing of these applications. Thus, the definition of UNIX is not simple or clear-cut. Rather, UNIX is a montage of tools and techniques designed to provide an efficient and optimal environment for the development and execution of programs and applications.

THE HISTORY OF UNIX

Though UNIX's history has been recounted many times, it is useful to examine that history again before studying the internals of UNIX. The history of UNIX provides many interesting insights into the philosophy of UNIX, which is an important underlying feature and influence upon the development of this rather remarkable operating system. Students of computer science and the computer industry understand that UNIX was influenced by many forces—some coming before its inception. Additionally, the techniques employed in the development of UNIX have influenced many subsequent industry products.

The first public description of UNIX came in a paper presented in 1974 in the journal *Communications of the ACM* by Ken Thompson and Dennis Ritchie. The growth and acceptance of UNIX since that paper has been steady. UNIX has progressed in status from that of a rather specialized and esoteric academic exercise to that of a well-received, multi-user operating system currently being touted as an industry standard. UNIX has been successfully ported from a single mini-computer to the complete range of hardware from micros to maxis, with virtually no port considered impossible or even ill advised.

Popular in colleges and universities from the start, UNIX is now popular in business and industry as well. The impact of its popularity in the academic world has been to provide an increasing number of graduates having UNIX experience. In addition, academic experimentation and enhancement has provided many extensions and improvements to the original versions which are now incorporated in the latest release of UNIX.

While the inception of UNIX itself is dated as being sometime in 1969, its real birth was in 1966. At that time Bell Laboratories, General Electric and the Massachusetts Institute of Technology joined forces to create an operating system which would provide simultaneous computer access to a large community of users (essentially a timesharing system). This system was to be called MULTICS. The MULTICS operating system became marginally operational in 1969. At this time, it also became clear to the powers that be that for a variety of reasons the objectives of the MULTICS project were going to be unmet. When the impending failure of the project became apparent, Bell Laboratories pulled out of it.

Even though Bell Labs took its people out of the project, it could not take the project away from the people. Among the participants on the project were Ken Thompson and Dennis Ritchie. Their participation on the MULTICS project and sensitization to the complexities of a timesharing system led them to produce a strictly on-paper design of the UNIX operating system in 1969.

Following this paper design, Ken Thompson began to write a series of programs which would simulate the behaviors described in the design. He did not begin by writing the overall operating system. Instead, his first attentions were given to simulating the behavior of a file system and executing programs in the demanding paging environment described in his design.

2

Thompson and Ritchie enjoyed playing games (albeit sophisticated ones) on and with the computer. In particular, the creation of an accurate orrery (a planetary motion simulation) was an area of fascination. The cost of running such a game on the large mainframes of the time was excessive however, and the display characteristics and file control provided in such an environment was unsatisfactory. When a DEC PDP-7 computer with some graphics capabilities became available to them, all Thompson and Ritchie needed for their project was the appropriate development and processing environment for the hardware. And so, the first version of UNIX, based upon the paper design, was implemented on a PDP-7.

The name UNIX was coined as a pun on MULTICS. The creation of this name is attributed to Brian Kernighan.

The influences affecting the creation of UNIX are worth noting. The initial goal of its developers, back on the MULTICS project, was to create a timesharing operating system. Thus, there was clear sensitivity to the needs of a fair processing distribution environment. The developers also needed an environment which provided the type of file system necessary for their particular interests—the orrery, and other projects that interested them. Finally, they needed a processing environment which was efficient enough to maximize the speed of processing. These factors were the driving influences on the initial development of the UNIX system.

In 1971, the UNIX system was ported to a PDP-11. This port was noteworthy because of the extremely small size of the complete operating system (less than 20k). Up until that time, standard practice was to write programs on another machine and then cross-compile them to the PDP series. Ken Thompson tried to implement a Fortran compiler under UNIX, but finally gave up and developed the language B. Largely influenced by BCPL (still in use in some areas), B was an interpretive language.

Interpretive languages failed to provide the wished-for performance, motivating Ritchie to evolve the compiled language C from B. Finally, in 1973, UNIX itself was rewritten in C.

In 1984 there were roughly 100,000 UNIX installations in existence, and that number is growing rapidly. Since UNIX is written in a high level language (C), it is fairly easy to read and understand, which makes for easy porting. It has been estimated that UNIX is perhaps one-third larger and slower than it needs to be because it is not written in a low level language. The benefits of the high level language clearly outweigh those that might be achieved from low level language, however.

UNIX'S POPULARITY

What factors make UNIX an increasingly popular choice in today's market? There are seven basic features which contribute to its growing acceptance.

The UNIX system provides a simple user interface. While those new to UNIX may question its simplicity, the experienced user can see that UNIX clearly does provide a consistent and straightforward user interface. Some of its commands are complex due to the amount of power and flexibility which they possess, but all commands follow the same general formatting rules and approaches.

The basic philosophy of UNIX is to provide and build tools which can then perform a vast spectrum of functions. Complex features and mechanisms are built upon simple tools. The primitives, or low level system functions or routines provided by UNIX yield an environment which is consistent with this building block or tool approach.

UNIX provides a *hierarchical file system*, which offers better file organization and ultimately faster response times. The basic description of a hierarchical file system is that it is one in which a tree-like structure provides "leaves" from a branch for the containment of files. These leaves are called *directories* or *subdirectories*. The common point from which all subdirectories spring is called the *root directory* (referred to as \). The root is the *parent* of all directories. Each parent directory can be said to have directories that are its children, or *child* directories. Any parent's child directories can have children of its own, and this branching off process can go on and on. The tree-structured directory process is limited only by hardware constraints. Each parent or child directory is basically just a table of the files that are contained within it. Thus, a typically structured UNIX directory might look like the drawing in Figure 0-1.

In addition to a hierarchical file system, UNIX provides a consistent, *byte stream* approach to all file handling. In a byte stream approach, every file and device is treated the same—simply as a mechanism for processing a stream of bytes in some manner. Thus, as far as the UNIX kernel is concerned, a disk drive looks and behaves just the same as a monitor or any data file, and all are treated the same by the kernel. This greatly simplifies kernel processing.

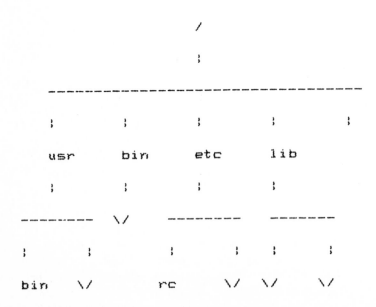

Fig. 0-1. Typical tree-structured UNIX directory.

The byte stream approach to file handling also permits a consistent approach to handling all peripheral devices. Peripherals like printers, disk drives and monitors are treated like data files. Any operation which can be performed on a file can thus ostensibly be performed on any peripheral. Special pieces of software called *device drivers* provide the interface between these devices and the kernel. The drivers can be rewritten and replaced or added as necessary to handle special cases or unusual devices.

UNIX is a true multi-user, multi-tasking environment. As such, multiple users can be supported efficiently even on a fairly small machine. UNIX is, at this time, the only significant operating system which can make this claim for small machines—while also providing an identical environment on large machines.

Finally, UNIX hides both hardware and machine architecture from the user and the programmer to a great degree. Programs and applications running in a UNIX environment on one machine can be moved to other machines and the intricacies involved in the hardware and machine language changes required for that move will be transparent to the users making the change.

For these reasons, UNIX continues to increase in popularity as an ideal operating system. It provides all the tools necessary for a sophisticated development environment as well as a complete and efficient application environment.

THE UNIX USER ENVIRONMENT

The UNIX environment has often been likened to an onion, where the various layers can be peeled away yielding a smaller and smaller whole until one reaches a non-reducible center. If we take this image, we will see that this onion we call UNIX has three significant layers around a non-reducible center. Although many additional layers could easily be added, these three layers are integral to the UNIX environment.

The center of the UNIX environment, and of any operating system environment is the hardware itself. The disk capacity, memory, processors and peripherals compose the center around which UNIX is built. The UNIX kernel in effect "covers" the hardware. The kernel is the real operating system part of UNIX and shields the user from the difficulties inherent in dealing directly with the hardware. The kernel is the non-removable part of UNIX. Without the kernel, UNIX would cease to exist as we know it. Around the kernel is the shell or shells. The shell provides the basic tools necessary for communicating with and using the operating system. If the kernel can be seen as shielding the user from the hardware, the shell, in effect, shields the user from the operating system kernel. The third necessary layer of the UNIX environment "rests" on the shell and is comprised of the *application programs*. These are the user-developed tools that make the operating system valuable in a business, scientific or engineering environment.

Among the many functions of the kernel, which will be discussed in this book, two stand out as key: the kernal provides the file system and the processing environment. It was these two features that Ken Thompson and

Dennis Ritchie knew they needed to develop when they started on the road to the creation of UNIX.

The UNIX file system provided by the kernel is a hierarchical, directory-based system in which everything is treated like a file. Files are just streams of bytes to be processed and that is exactly how the kernel views them, without regard to their source or destination. In addition, the directories driving the hierarchical structure are themselves ordinary files. By treating absolutely everything as if it were just another file, the kernel enforces extraordinary consistency throughout the file system.

UNIX offers more than just the consistent treatment of files in a hierarchical environment. Files can be created and deleted, have thorough access protection and grow dynamically. As files are created, they are given various protections that determine who can read, write and execute those files. When a file is updated or extended, a table of blocks is updated so that non-contiguous disk blocks can be used to store the file, even if it grows.

A program is nothing more than a file whose bytes contain the information necessary to trigger the proper results when executing. In this sense, a program is a file which can be executed. A *process* is an instance of an executing program. The UNIX kernel is capable of handling simultaneously executing processes. It allows processes to be created (for example, by loading a program file) and terminated. It also controls communications between processes and synchronizes the various process events as necessary.

Processes in the UNIX environment operate on one of two levels—either the user level or the kernel level. Whenever a user process needs operating or kernel services (such as communications with another process), a *system call* is made. The system call is a request for operating system services. The kernel processes all such requests. Users can never directly access these kernel functions, but must issue system calls to do so. The kernel operates on behalf of the user to provide hardware and other resources not normally available to the user.

The kernel is therefore the driver of the UNIX system. It interfaces with the hardware to provide a file system, a process execution environment, and to deal with all of the hardware, coordination, and synchronization issues associated with the file system and process execution.

The shell provides user services from the kernel. Two of the major features provided by the kernel are redirection and piping. With the use of piping, the output of one process is provided as the input to another simultaneously executing process. The following example illustrates the use of a shell pipe:

```
$ ls *.doc₄wc −1
```

In this example, both ls (which provides a directory listing of the current directory), and wc (which provides a character, line, and word count) are simultaneously executed for the user. The kernel synchronizes these processes so that wc waits for its input from ls. Thus ls *.doc, which would normally provide a directory list of all files with a .doc extension, directs its output to a pipeline. The other end of this pipeline is the input to wc. The −l parameters tells wc to count lines of input.

In piping, the standard output of a process is redirected to an open pipeline where it is used as standard input. In a similar manner, standard input and standard output can be redirected to files by the kernel. The operator causes standard output to be redirected, while the operator causes standard input to be redirected. In all cases, redirection and piping in the shell is responsible for requesting that the kernel change the file descriptor of the affected standard input and standard output to point to the pipeline or named file.

The shell has the task of interpreting the command lines and causing the execution of the correct programs and the appropriate parsing of command parameters. The shell is also traditionally viewed as containing the basic UNIX commands such as ed, grep, ls, cat and so on. The shell may be peeled away and replaced as is indicated by the usage of the system.

Application programs run using hardware resources requested on their behalf by the kernel, and in the environment established by the kernel, only after they have been correctly submitted for execution by the shell. Thus, the picture of UNIX as an onion holds rather well—perhaps too well. During the course of this book layers of UNIX will be gradually peeled away to reveal its many complexities. At times this process may seem sufficiently painful to bring tears to your eyes, but with care, perseverance, and proper paring, the onion will be peeled, and pain will be kept to a minimum.

UNIX Flaws

With these strengths and features, the question may be asked "Why doesn't everyone use UNIX?" The answer to this question is important for two reasons. First, it indicates future directions for the UNIX operating system to grow, develop and evolve. Second, it shows where UNIX is weak and not ideally suited to all applications.

In general, one of UNIX's weaknesses is its age. It has been evolving since 1969 and so is a relatively old software product. With age many of the bugs have been worked out so age is not entirely negative. However, the state of data processing technology when UNIX was first developed influenced its fundamental concepts. The line by line rather than full screen orientation of UNIX is a result of the teletype terminals in use when UNIX was first built. More and more products and modifications are appearing to work around this line at a time view of the world, but the fundamental weakness is still there.

Another drawback, stemming both from age and from the laboratory development environment, is the extremely unfriendly user interface. Error messages like "Panic: Core dumped" and "Cannot fork" are not good for the naive user. In 1969 there were very few naive users of any type of computer and there were no naive users in the labs where UNIX was developed.

Besides these user interface flaws, there are several types of application for which UNIX is poorly suited. Its nature as a fair timesharing system makes it a poor choice for real-time applications. It may be a good if difficult fit for parallel processing applications (see discussion in Appendix C). On small, single user micros UNIX is so large that it is usually a poor choice unless portability is a crucial issue.

Summary

By design, UNIX is a programmers operating system. It provides computing resources fairly to a large community of users and comes with a rich set of tools. The tools UNIX provides are separate from the kernel (the operating system proper). Thus, the kernel can be kept small requiring less memory than equivalently powerful operating systems.

UNIX with its strengths, is not without flaws. It is not the answer to all problems. The rest of this book helps to clarify where and why UNIX is both strong and weak.

Points to Ponder

What is the optimal functional content of the kernel? How much functionality should be built into the kernel and how much should be removable? What are the impacts of increasing and decreasing the size of the kernel?

What can and should be done with the UNIX user interface? What direction should future enhancements to UNIX take?

The Process Image

One of the first obstacles in understanding the internals of the UNIX operation system, is understanding the language used in describing UNIX. Throughout this book many new terms and concepts will be introduced. The first of these terms is process. A process in UNIX is a running program. A program is the compiled, assembled or interpreted code which a programmer would write.

The *process image* is most simply defined as the picture of a process, made up of the information necessary to run a program. The process image is invisible to the user, but it is an important part of the UNIX environment, and comes into play when a program is to be executed. Consistent with the UNIX philosophy, programs are stored as byte streams. Each program's byte stream is a unique configuration of bytes and the protection flags associated with programs. In order to execute a program, an executable file is loaded into memory.

Each unique executable file (a file is executable after the source code is compiled or assembled) is loaded into memory as a process image. The process image, or picture of the process, remains in memory until it is time for the process image to run. At the time that the process image runs, it becomes a process. At this point, there is, in effect, a change in status of the process image. When in memory, the information that makes up a process is actually a process image. When executing from memory as a program running in the UNIX environment, the process image becomes a process. This distinction may seem trivial, but its importance will be demonstrated as the concept becomes more clearly delineated.

This chapter describes the structure of the process image and the process. It describes how the program is mapped from disk into memory, and in general terms how a process executes and accesses the kernel once it is loaded.

PROCESS CREATION

When a program is written, generally through the use of an editor, it comes into being as a source file. This source file is a sequence of bytes, still intelligible to human beings, which can be converted into an instruction set for the processor by means of a compiler. The simple C program hello.c, shown in Fig. 1-1 is an example of source code.

The task of compiling a C program in the UNIX environment is accomplished by the program cc. Compiling a program produces an executable file called a.out (of course, the compiler has options which allow a different name to be specified). Using the hello.c program as an example, the process of compiling and executing a program is illustrated in Fig. 1-2.

The executable file a.out is stored on disk with at least four distinct sections. These sections are the *header*, the *text segment*, the *data segment*, and the *symbol table*. If debugging options have been included a fifth section containing debugging information will be on disk as well.

The header contains information pertinent to the loading and actual execution of the file. Included in this information is the location and size of the additional data and the *stack space* necessary at execution time. Stack space is the part of the memory associated with a process that is usually used to contain local variables, parameters for and from function calls and other transient data related to processes.

The text segment contains protected code. This is typically the actual instructions contained in the source file converted to their machine instruction form.

Initialized data is contained in the data segment. This includes all static and external data types in a C program. Thus, when a static variable is declared in a C program, space is allocated for this variable in the data segment. The data in this area is modifiable by the program, but the space is permanently allocated.

The symbol table contains references to all symbols (literals) used in the program. All of those sections of a program containing information in quotes as well as other literals are placed in the symbol table. The construction of a.out as it exists on the disk is illustrated in Fig. 1-3.

Once an executable file has been created, the UNIX fork( ) call causes memory to be allocated and formatted for its execution. The exec( ) call causes the

```
main()
{
        printf("hello, world\n");
}
```

Fig. 1-1. Source code for hello.c.

```
$ cc hello.c
$ ls

hello.c
a.out
$ a.out

hello, world
$
```

Fig. 1-2. Compiling and executing a program.

executable code to be loaded from the disk into the allocated memory space. At the time the exec( ) call is issued the executable file changes and is transmuted into a process image in memory. This event is actually more of a copy than a change. The executable file is also retained on disk and is not itself modified. Rather, at this point both the executable file and something new called the process image co-exist. When the process image is actually executed, it becomes a process and another form of the same thing comes into being, since a process is defined as the execution of a process image.

This transition from source code to process is illustrated in Fig. 1-4.

The process image is stored either in memory or in a secondary storage area. A process image is constructed of four regions. These regions are the *code region* or *text region*, the *data region* and the *stack region*.

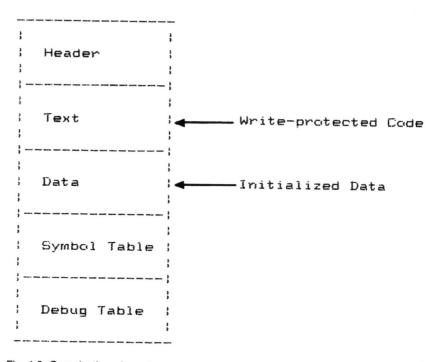

Fig. 1-3. Organization of a.out.

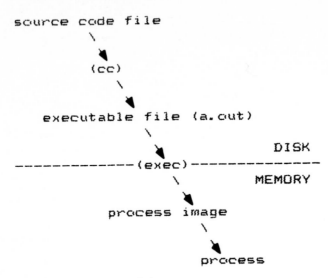

Fig. 1-4. Transition of the source code to a.

The kernel performs many functions for a process. It must always be able to run as required and as requested. Thus, a process, as it runs, tracks not only its own data, but the data of the kernel as the kernel performs on behalf of the process.

When a process executes, it must maintain and control both user information and system information. The system (or kernel) information cannot be directly accessed or manipulated by the user. It must be requested by means of system calls. A process is composed of unique code, data and stack regions for the user and the system. Figure 1-5 illustrates the general organization of a process.

On the kernel side, these three regions have operating system-oriented functions. The code region contains operating system code necessary for the execution of the particular process. The data region contains data structures or tables which the operating system needs. Interrupts, traps and system calls are stored in the kernel stack region.

The division between the kernel and user sides of process organization is crucial to the organization of the UNIX operating system. User requests for system information are allowed only through system calls. This is part of the "shielding" for which UNIX is renowned.

Once an exec( ) has been issued for a process, a portion of the kernel data area known as the kernel process table has an entry made in it for the new process image. This entry in the kernel process table indicates a new address in the u (for user) area which in turn points to a *per process region table*. Each process has its own table, or per process region table containing information about the particular process's address. The u area contains the important information about each process, including the size and location of the various regions.

The size of process regions is referred to in terms of *clicks*. A click is the

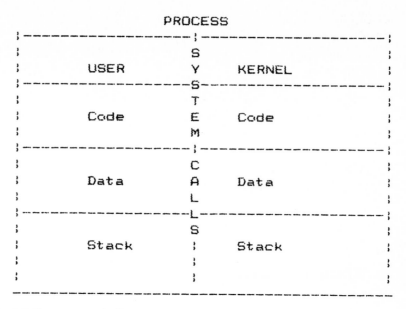

Fig. 1-5. Process organization.

smallest unit of memory which may be allocated. As processes are loaded and unloaded, or moved to secondary memory, the memory required is referred to in terms of the *page*. A page is the smallest amount of memory required for memory protection. A page is always a multiple of clicks. On a DEC VAX a page is the same size as a click.

On the user side a process image is organized into its three regions of code, data and stack. Each of these regions contains both used and unused space. In particular, the data area consists of an initialized region and an uninitialized region, referred to as *bss*. (The initials bss stand for "block started by symbol" and refer to an Assembly language pseudo operator used on the IBM 7090.) A picture of the process image's structure is shown in Fig. 1-6.

In the u area, u_tsize, u_dsize, and u_ssize contain the size in clicks of the code, data and stack areas respectively. The address of the first byte beyond the end of the unused code area is stored in etext. The address of the first byte beyond the bss is stored in end, while the address of the first byte beyond the initialized data area is stored in edata. The variable sp contains the address of the first byte beyond the unused stack area.

Each of the three areas has a distinct function for the process. The text area contains the write-protected code. Since this is write-protected code it is therefore not modifiable. Non-modifiable code for programs is the default for UNIX System V. This convention permits the shared text processing which increases efficiency by reducing redundant loading.

When code is not write-protected it is included in the data area. Non-write protected code is useful when self-modifying code is desired or desirable. In UNIX the *linker* (ld) assigns *magic numbers* (numbers which indicate special

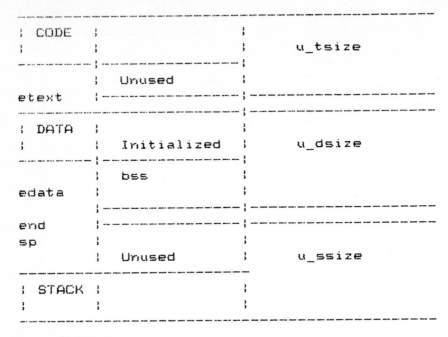

Fig. 1-6. Organization of process image.

or unique meanings) to these two types of code. The default write-protected code is referred to as a *410 a.out* (shared text). The non-write protected code is a *407 a.out*. An illustration of 407 a.out is included in Fig. 1-7.

The data area provides the stores for many of the variables used during program execution. The initialized data area contains *static data* (that is, data contained in locations which do not change during program execution). The "static" and "external" data types in C are stored in the initialized data area. This space is allocated at program load time. This is the data segment of the process image.

The data area also contains the bss or *dynamic storage area*. The memory used for this area is often referred to as the *heap*. It is an area of memory to which data access is not strictly last-in first-out or any other rigid pattern. This area is used to store the data created during C *malloc* and *calloc* calls (and all other calls which use the *sbrk( )* system call). This heap space is allocated at program execution time.

The stack area is a strictly structured area of memory. Information is stored on the stack on a last-in first-out basis. The stack is used to store "automatic" C variables, function parameters, and the values of saved registers. The life span of data stored in the stack area is the same as that of the particular function being executed which is to say that data lasts in the stack area as long as the function is executed. The allocation of stack space occurs at execution time and stack space is deallocated and reallocated as functions are invoked and exited.

The stack works by pushing on logical stack frames as functions are invoked and popping these stack frames off as functions are exited. This can

14

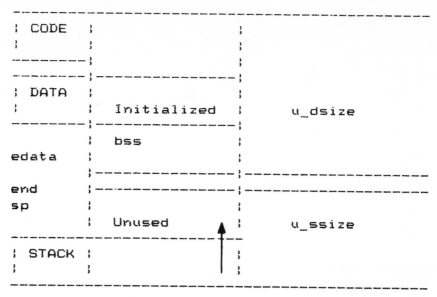

Fig. 1-7. 407 a.out.

be more clearly described if you imagine each piece of data as a poker chip, organized into a logical order. The first poker chip to be acted upon is placed on the top of the stack of chips. The next chip to be acted upon is placed on top of the first chip, which in effect "pushes" that initial first chip down one slot. When the data is required for use, the data, or chips, are taken from the top, or "popped" off the stack. The stack pointer, which is a special register, tracks the depth of a stack during execution.

Note that in Fig. 1-7 it appears that the stack is in fact growing up (from low to high memory) and in many cases this is true. This is important to programmers because if insufficient stack space and/or bss area is available during execution it is possible for the two areas to intrude on each other. In particular, if many calls for dynamic memory allocation are made (malloc calls), it is possible for the bss to expand into the stack space. Execution (or run time) errors of many kinds may occur when this happens.

SYSTEM CALLS

Both user and kernel modes of execution have independent stack space. System calls provide the interface between the user and kernel areas. System calls are contained in a special system call library. When a system call is made, its entry point to the system call library is found. When the system call library is entered an interrupt occurs which causes a literal hardware switch to the kernel mode.

Once the kernel mode has been entered, the kernel code, data, and stack are used instead of the user code, data, or stack. The system call request is processed and when complete, another hardware switch back to user mode is performed. Once the process is executing in user mode again, the kernel stack of the process is null. Thus, the kernel functions are protected and controlled by the use of system calls.

OF INTEREST TO PROGRAMMERS

The key points in this chapter for programmers are the differences between 407 and 410 a.out models, the times at which the various regions of memory are allocated and the effect of stack and heap growth on each other. These points are summarized below.

The 407 a.out model combines code and data, while the 410 a.out model distinguishes the code and data areas. In the 407 a.out model, the code as part of the data area is accessible for writing while the process is executing. Thus in this model a program could modify its own code and behavior as it executed.

The 410 a.out model protects the code segment so that it cannot be modified. However, since it is certain that the code will not change if multiple occurrences of the same process are running, the code portion will be loaded only one time for all the processes. After it has been loaded once it will be reused by any other processes needing it. The 410 a.out allows more efficient memory usage, faster loading of multiple occurrences of the same process and generally more effective use of system resources.

The times during execution and loading of a process when memory for the various process areas is allocated are shown in Fig. 1-8.

Smaller programs will load more quickly, so if load time is a factor in your programming, you will want to program so that the initialized data area is minimized while the bss is maximized. Unfortunately, the clarity of code associated with programs with a large bss in favor of small initialized data areas is often poor. In addition, care must be taken to allow sufficient growth of the stack area if a large bss is desired.

The growth of the stack and the size of the bss must be considered during design, writing and compilation of a program, since all of these phases can affect the potential conflicts between these two areas. In a system where the stack grows down, potential conflicts with the bss are less likely.

Summary

Source code which has been assembled or compiled and is currently executed is a process. When the process is resident in memory, but is not running it is called a process image. This process image is a loded version of the executable code stored on the disk.

A process image consists of four areas, the header, the text, the data, and the symbol table. The data is comprised of stack and bss (or heap space). Care should be taken not to allow the stack and the bss to intrude on each other as memory is allocated while a program is running. Should such an intrusion occur—unpredictable results will occur.

The text of a process may be either protected or unprotected. When text is protected it can be used in shared text processing, whereby multiple copies of the same process can all share the same text portion. In non-shared mode, when the text is unprotected, the text is actually a portion of the data. Programs

```
;--------------------------------------------------;
;                         ;                        ;
; Program Load            ; Execution              ;
; Allocation              ; Allocation             ;
;-------------------------;------------------------;
;                         ;                        ;
;                         ;                        ;
; Code Area               ; bss Area               ;
;                         ;                        ;
; Initialized             ; Stack Area             ;
;    Data Area            ;                        ;
;                         ;                        ;
;--------------------------------------------------;
```

Fig. 1-8. Memory allocation times.

which are self-modifying take advantage of this organization to change executions instructions while running.

Points to Ponder

When would you want to use non-protected text mode? What are the reasonable applications for self-modifiable code?

Would you make kernel modifications to ensure that the stack and the bss cannot intrude on each other? What would the impact and implications of such modifications be?

2

CPU Scheduling

UNIX is a timesharing operating system. As such it must have a way to allow each user the illusion that they have a complete computer to themselves. Since there is only a single processor in each UNIX system, only one process can actually run at a time. This means that processes must be activated and deactivated with efficiency, and that this must be done in a "fair" manner, so that processes are given as much time as they need to run when they need to run.

Scheduling Overview

The issues associated with scheduling CPU resources can be quite complex. The ability to fairly share CPU resources is critical to any operating system environment. There are two basic philosophies relating to CPU resource scheduling—straight line and round robin.

Straight line scheduling provides CPU resources to each process or activity in order, staying with that activity until it is complete. This is the type of scheduling that goes in a single user environment. Each task is completed in order. If a process does get interrupted, it must be restarted. This is not the philosophy followed by UNIX.

The other approach to scheduling is a round robin scheduler where processes and activities are preempted in order to allow other processes and activities to run. While no single process will complete as quickly using the round robin approach, the CPU user is more fairly distributed from a user viewpoint.

UNIX uses round robin scheduling with multilevel feedback. Under this philosophy processes run for preset amounts of time until they either complete or are preempted to allow another process to run. Once a process is preempted it is placed on a run queue where it goes through one or more levels of run priority evaluation and update. The process on the run queue with the highest priority is always the next to run. When a preempted process is selected to run again, it will resume executing where it left off.

Preemptive scheduling and process controls are critical in UNIX. Preemption means that a process which has not completed execution can be interrupted by the kernel. Once interrupted it must be restartable.

Process preemption is another complex and critical area affecting CPU scheduling. For scheduling to be fair, preemption must be possible. For preemption to be an effective tool, it must be non-destructive. Thus, at preemption a context switch occurs. This context switch saves the context of the currently running and now preempted process and restores the context of the process to be started. The context is essentially a snapshot of the system and process environments at the time of preemption. The snapshot includes the contents of the user address space (the user area), the hardware registers, and the kernel data structures. This data is saved as the context of the process and when it is restored the process can resume execution as if nothing had happened.

Finally, in order to be fair about scheduling CPU resources the sequence in which processes are chosen to run must be equitable. In the UNIX environment scheduling is based upon priorities. The highest priority process is always the next to run. Priority is based on several factors: CPU usage, base priority, user assigned priority adjustments (nice values). The most important criteria are base priority and CPU usage. Kernel processes always have high base priorities and thus always have the opportunity to run first and longest. UNIX is heavily biased against CPU bound processes, so processes which have relatively low CPU usages will receive the most opportunity to run. The key factor in understanding this is that when a process requests I/O it will generally go to sleep and relinquish the CPU thus keeping its CPU usage low even though by the clock on the wall it may have been running for a long time.

UNIX TIMING

The clock on a UNIX system runs in a way that creates an interrupt many times a second. The exact number of interrupts per second is hardware-dependent. On an AT&T 3B-type computer for example, the clock interrupts occur 100 times per second. The one second measure is an important unit in UNIX. A one-second interval is known as a quantum or a time slice.

Every process is allocated a one-second quantum in which to run. Thus, no process is able to run uninterrupted for more than one second. At the end of a quantum, the running process is stopped or preempted and all processes waiting to execute (as process images) are analyzed to determine which one should run next. A process may terminate its running status before the one second time slice allocated to it is used, but it can never get more than a single time slice without interruption. It is sometimes possible for the process which has just been preempted to run again immediately.

Clock Interrupt Handler

The terms clock interrupt and clock tick are synonymous in the UNIX environment. As was just described, all timing in the UNIX system is based on these clock interrupts or ticks. The clock interrupt handler is the system software that processes the clock ticks. It is a small, interruptible piece of software which runs very fast and at a very high priority. Because of its speed, construction, and priority, the periods when other processes are blocked by the clock interrupt handler are very small. The clock interrupt handler performs several functions.

First, when the clock interrupt occurs the clock generally stops, so the handler must restart the clock so that timing can continue. Failure to restart the clock would result in no further system timing occurring so scheduling would be impossible.

Several kernel functions are required on a real time or pseudo real time basis. In particular, certain I/O functions necessitate the activation of functions within ticks of particular events. This real time processing is built into the clock interrupt handler. It schedules the start of these kernel functions based on internal timers.

The interrupt handler is responsible for profiling and statistics gathering on process execution. It does the execution profiling and gathers the system and accounting statistics. Basic time tracking is handled in this piece of software as is the sending of time based alarm signals.

Finally, the clock interrupt handler has the task of waking the swapper at least once each second of controlling process scheduling.

Process Context

When a process is preempted, the status of that process must be saved so that it can later be restored and its execution resumed at exactly the place it was stopped. The *context of a process* is all the necessary information about a running process which is needed for that process to run properly and to continue running properly. When a process is preempted, its context is saved.

A process context consists of *user area information*, *register information*, and *system information*. All of this information is stored at the time of process preemption. When a process is moved to running status, this information is restored so that the process may continue running as if it had never stopped.

The user area information which must be stored is the code, the data and the stack as they were described in the previous chapter. In addition, any shared memory must be stored at the time of context saving.

There are four types of register information to be stored. First, the *program counter* register value is stored. The program counter specifies the next instruction to be executed. The *process status*, which contains the hardware status at the time of preemption is stored. The third register stored is the *stack pointer*. This register contains the current address of the next entry in the *kernel stack* or *user stack*. Whether the user or kernel stack is referenced depends on the mode of operation at the time of preemption. Other information is stored in the *general purpose register*, which is the place where arguments and local variables are stored.

The system information to be stored is of two types: *static information* and *dynamic information*. The static information about a process context stays with that process throughout the process's life, but the dynamic parts of the process context may vary in size and number as the process goes through various phases. The *process table* entry is part of the static system information about a process. The information contained in the process table includes the CPU status, the memory status, the amount of time the process has been resident in memory, the CPU usage of the process, its priority class, and its priority.

System user area information, which makes up another portion of the static system information, includes a pointer to the current directory, a pointer to the root directory, the effective user I.D., the save area for the CPU registers, and arguments for the system call. The final portions of the static system information are the region and per process region tables which are used by the memory management facilities to map from virtual to physical addresses.

The dynamic portion of the system information should be viewed as a series of *context layers*. These layers consist of two parts: the kernel stack for a process as it executes in kernel mode and the information necessary for each layer to recover the previous layer. These various layers come into being as interrupts and system calls occur. The maximum number of layers will exist if a series of interrupts occurs in a "worst case" way during the execution of a system call.

Once the time has come for a process to be preempted, the context as illustrated in Figure 2-1 is saved. When a process is running, this context is an up-to-date reflection of all the information necessary to the accurate execution of the process.

THE SWITCHER

In the *system code area* there exists a subroutine called swtch( ). This subroutine is referred to as the *switcher*. It is the task of the switcher to remove a process from running status, save its context and restore another process to running status. The switcher subroutine is called by the running process. It is called voluntarily (for a number of possible reasons as will be seen later) or involuntarily because the one second time slice has elapsed.

The UNIX operating system maintains a *run queue*. The run queue is a logical view of the process table in which the only entries are those that can be run. The run queue is a singly-linked list. The process table entry p__link points to the next entry in the run queue. Entries are pushed onto the run queue, so that the entry runq, which points to the head of the run queue always points

```
 ---------------------------------------
 ;                                     ;
 ;              User Level             ;
 ;       ------------------------      ;
 ;       ;       Text        ;        ;
 ;       ;-------------------;        ;
 ;       ;       Data        ;        ;
 ;       ;-------------------;        ;
 ;       ;      Stack        ;        ;
 ;       ;    (Registers)    ;        ;
 ;       ;  ---------------   ;        ;
 ;       ;  ; Program   ;   ;        ;
 ;       ;  ; Counter   ;   ;        ;
 ;       ;  ;-----------;   ;        ;
 ;       ;  ; Processor;   ;        ;
 ;       ;  ; Status    ;   ;        ;
 ;       ;  ;-----------;   ;        ;
 ;       ;  ; Stack     ;   ;        ;
 ;       ;  ; Pointer   ;   ;        ;
 ;       ;  ;-----------;   ;        ;
 ;       ;  ; General   ;   ;        ;
 ;       ;  ; Purpose   ;   ;        ;
 ;       ;   ---------------   ;        ;
 ;       ------------------------      ;
 ;                                     ;
 ;             System Level            ;
 ;               (Static)              ;
 ;       ------------------------      ;
 ;       ;      Process       ;        ;
 ;       ;      Table         ;        ;
 ;       ;      Entries       ;        ;
 ;       ;-------------------;        ;
 ;       ;      User          ;        ;
 ;       ;      Area          ;        ;
 ;       ;      Entries       ;        ;
 ;       ;-------------------;        ;
 ;       ;      Region        ;        ;
 ;       ;      Table         ;        ;
 ;       ;      Entries       ;        ;
 ;       ------------------------      ;
 ;                                     ;
```

Fig. 2-1. Process context.

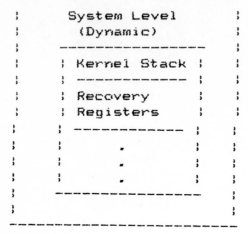

```
  }       System Level        }    }
  }         (Dynamic)         }    }
  }    ------------------     }    }
  }    } Kernel Stack }       }    }
  }    } ----------- }        }    }
  }    } Recovery    }        }    }
  }    } Registers   }        }    }
  }    } ----------- }        }    }
  }    }        .    }        }    }
  }    }        .    }        }    }
  }    }        .    }        }    }
  }    ------------------     }    }
  }                                }
  ----------------------------------
```

Fig. 2-1. Continued.

to the process most recently added to the run queue. This is illustrated in Fig. 2-2.

The task of swtch( ) is to take the currently running process and return it to the run queue, and take a process from the run queue and make it the running process. It does these things by performing the following steps:

☐ Saves the context of the running process (the save( ) routine handles the task of saving the registers).
☐ Selects the process in the run queue which has the highest priority.
☐ Removes the selected process from the run queue.
☐ Makes the selected process the running process. This restoration of context entails the remapping of the user structures and the system stack to the system virtual address space.
☐ Restores the registers of the selected process (the resumea( ) routine handles the task of restoring registers which have been saved using the save( ) routine).

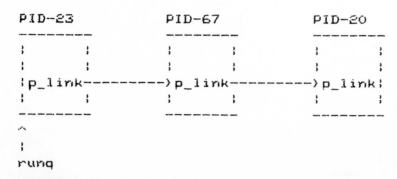

Fig. 2-2. Run queue header and linkage.

24

It may seem as though a tremendous amount of activity is occurring at least once a second, and in some sense it is. However, the saving and restoring of process context requires no physical relocation of any data. All that is occurring during these moments is the changing of addresses so that the part of the kernel responsible for actually running the process has the appropriate addresses and registers to access. This should be of special interest to programmers and system administrators.

PROCESS PRIORITY

While swtch( ) is responsible for selecting the next process to run from the run queue, it must have some fair mechanism for making this choice. The process table contains an entry called p__pri. This p__pri entry contains the current priority of a process. Processes can have priorities ranging from 0 (meaning a process which must be run) to 119 (a process waiting for death). The lower the priority number of a process, the higher its actual priority and the more likely it is to be selected to be run. The priority of every process in the run queue is computed once every second, except for the running process which has its priority updated every clock tick or time slice. In general terms, the priority of a process is based on the ratio of required compute time (CPU usage) to elapsed time on the queue (resident time), as well as on the process's priority class.

When swtch( ) operates, it will always select the highest priority item from the run queue. In the case of equal priorities, the process furthest from runq (the most recent run queue entry) will be selected. This is shown in Fig. 2-3. Note that PID stands for process I.D. number, and pri is priority.

This figure shows a run queue with priorities attached. In this example, the process with PID 67 would be selected by swtch( ) since its priority number (61) is the lowest of the group, making it of the highest priority in the run queue. If the currently running process was added to the run queue with PID 45, the new run queue might appear as illustrated in Fig. 2-4.

The most important factor in determining the priority of a process is the ratio of compute time versus elapsed time. This ratio is stored in a process

```
  PID-23                 PID-67                 PID-20
 --------               --------               --------
:pri=67:               :pri=61:               :pri=80:
:       :               :       :               :       :
:p_link----------->p_link----------->p_link:
:       :               :       :               :       :
 --------               --------               --------
   .^.
    :
  runq
```

Fig. 2-3. Run queue with priorities.

```
PID-45                  PID-23                  PID-20
--------                --------                --------
!pri=80!                !pri=62!                !pri=70!
!       !               !       !               !       !
!p_link---------->p_link---------->p_link!
!       !               !       !               !       !
--------                --------                --------
^
!
runq
```

Fig. 2-4. New run queue with priorities.

table field called p_cpu. In practice it works out that p_cpu is a count of the amount of CPU usage required by the process, which is effectively the measure of the compute time/elapsed time ratio. Processes which are I/O bound are clearly favored in this formula over processes which are CPU bound. Suppose, for example, that a process needs a lot of user input (an order entry type of program, for example). While waiting for the keyboard data, a process such as this would normally be sleeping while waiting for input. Thus, even though it had a long elapsed time, it would have used very little CPU time and would therefore have a lower p_cpu then a process which was very CPU intensive.

In addition to the p_cpu value, priority is based on priority class which is recorded in the process table entry p_nice. The p_nice value is a secondary factor in computing priorities. Values in this entry can range from 0 to 39 with the default value being 20. The p_nice values of 0 to 9 are reserved for the superuser. The nice( ) system call can be used to change the p_nice value for a process. However, while anyone can increase a p_nice value with a nice( ) call, only the superuser can decrease p_nice values.

The actual computation of priorities is performed as follows. First, the p_cpu value is incremented every tick of the running process. Thus, for a process never run before, starting with a p_cpu value of 0 and assuming a clock which ticked 60 times per second, the p_cpu value would start at 0 and increment to 60 at the end of its time slice.

At the end of each time slice the p_cpu value for all processes, including the process which had been running is divided by 2. Thus, every second

$$p\_cpu = p\_cpu / 2$$

Also during every second all process priorites are recomputed except for those processes already having system priority (that is, priority levels from 0 to 40; system priorities are not recomputed). Note that system priority and system mode are not the same. A process in system mode may well have a priority above 40, but a process with priority below 40 will always be in system mode.

26

In the computation of priorities, two constants are used: the *base priority* called *PUSER* and the *nice zero constant* called *NZERO*. For user processes, PUSER is 60, and NZERO is 20. After p_cpu is recomputed each second, the priority (stored in p_pri) is recomputed using the following formula:

p_pri = (p_cpu / 2) + PUSER + (p_nice – NZERO)

Thus, after one second, a new user process would have a p_pri equal to:

p_cpu = 30 = 60 / 2

p_pri = 75 = (30 / 2) + 60 + (20 – 20)

There is one restriction on the incrementing of p_cpu. This value is never allowed to exceed 80. Therefore, if the same process were selected to run again immediately (perhaps because no other jobs were in the run queue) then its priority at the end of another second would be:

PUSER = 60

p_cpu = 40 = 80 / 2

p_pri = 80 = (40 / 2) + 60 + (20 – 20)

While swtch( ) selects the next process to run, and is responsible for the saving of the context of the currently running process, it does not add the currently running process to the run queue. Another process called qswtch( ) actually adds a process to the run queue. Thus, a process preempted before completion is added to the run queue and made available for later running by means of the qswtch( ) routine.

We will now examine two cases of running processes to see how process priorities are determined. For the sake of convenience, in both examples, which are a series of figures, the following assumptions are in force:

☐ there are exactly four processes.
☐ all processes are runnable at all times (they are not sleeping).
☐ all processes would run forever.
☐ there are 60 clock ticks per second.

Figures 2-5 through 2-15 illustrates the case in which all processes have the same p_nice value.

The process with p_id = 8 is selected to run since it is farthest from the run queue header (runq).

The second example shown in Figures 2-16 through 2-24 illustrates the case in which the processes have different nice values. We will also assume that they start with different priorities.

```
  -----------------     -----------------     -----------------     -----------------
  !  p_id   = 5  !      !  p_id   = 6  !      !  p_id   = 7  !      !  p_id   = 8  !
  !  p_cpu  = 0  !      !  p_cpu  = 0  !      !  p_cpu  = 0  !      !  p_cpu  = 0  !
  !  p_pri  = 60 !      !  p_pri  = 60 !      !  p_pri  = 60 !      !  p_pri  = 60 !
  !  p_nice = 20 !      !  p_nice= 20  !      !  p_nice= 20  !      !  p_nice= 20  !
  !  p_link = ---!----)!  p_link=----!----)!  p_link=----!----)!  p_link= 0   !
  !              !      !              !      !              !      !              !
  -----------------     -----------------     -----------------     -----------------
  ^
  !
  runq
```

Fig. 2-5. Run queue at start of example.

```
  -----------------
  !   p_id   = 8  !
  !  0<=p_cpu<=60 !
  !   p_pri  = 60 !
  !   p_nice = 20 !
  !   p_link = 0  !
  !               !
  -----------------
```

Running Process

```
  -------------------       -------------------       -------------------
  !   p_id   = 5   !        !   p_id   = 6   !        !   p_id   = 7   !
  !   p_cpu  = 0   !        !   p_cpu = 0    !        !   p_cpu = 0    !
  !   p_pri  = 60  !        !   p_pri = 60   !        !   p_pri = 60   !
  !   p_nice = 20  !        !   p_nice= 20   !        !   p_nice= 20   !
  !   p_link = ---!----->!  p_link=-----!----->!  p_link= 0    !
  !               !        !               !        !               !
  -------------------       -------------------       -------------------
  ^
  !
  runq
```

Fig. 2-6. Run queue and running process.

```
  -----------------     -----------------     -----------------     -----------------
  !  p_id   = 8  !      !  p_id   = 5  !      !  p_id   = 6  !      !  p_id   = 7  !
  !  p_cpu  = 30 !      !  p_cpu  = 0  !      !  p_cpu = 0   !      !  p_cpu = 0   !
  !  p_pri  = 75 !      !  p_pri  = 60 !      !  p_pri  = 60 !      !  p_pri  = 60 !
  !  p_nice = 20 !      !  p_nice= 20  !      !  p_nice= 20  !      !  p_nice= 20  !
  !  p_link = ---!----)!  p_link=----!----)!  p_link=----!----)!  p_link= 0   !
  !              !      !              !      !              !      !              !
  -----------------     -----------------     -----------------     -----------------
  ^
  !
  runq
```

Fig. 2-7. Run queue after one second.

28
```
```

```
 ------------------
 |   p_id    = 7   |
 |  0 <=p_cpu <=60 |
 |   p_pri   = 60  |
 |   p_nice = 20   |
 |   p_link = 0    |
 |                 |
 ------------------
```

Running Process

```
 ------------------      ------------------      ------------------
 |   p_id    = 8   |      |   p_id    = 5   |      |   p_id    = 6   |
 |   p_cpu  = 30   |      |   p_cpu = 0     |      |   p_cpu = 0     |
 |   p_pri   = 75  |      |   p_pri  = 60   |      |   p_pri = 60    |
 |   p_nice = 20   |      |   p_nice= 20    |      |   p_nice= 20    |
 |   p_link  = ---|----->|  p_link=----|---->|  p_link= 0      |
 |                 |      |                 |      |                 |
 ------------------      ------------------      ------------------
 ^
 |
 runq
```

Fig. 2-8. Run queue and running process during second second.

```
 ------------------      ------------------      ------------------      ------------------
 |  p_id    = 7   |      |  p_id   = 8    |      |  p_id    = 5   |      |  p_id   = 6    |
 |  p_cpu   = 30  |      |  p_cpu  = 15   |      |  p_cpu = 0     |      |  p_cpu = 0     |
 |  p_pri   = 75  |      |  p_pri = 67    |      |  p_pri  = 60   |      |  p_pri = 60    |
 |  p_nice = 20   |      |  p_nice= 20    |      |  p_nice= 20    |      |  p_nice= 20    |
 |  p_link = ---|----->|  p_link=----|---->|  p_link=----|---->|  p_link= 0     |
 |                |      |                |      |                |      |                |
 ------------------      ------------------      ------------------      ------------------
 ^
 |
 runq
```

Fig. 2-9. Run queue after 2 seconds.

The process with p_id = 6 is selected to run since it has the highest initial priority.

Note in this second example the tremendous impact of the various p_nice values. Process 5 gets a great deal of run time because of its p_nice of 10, while process 7 will not run until all of the other processes are complete because of its p_nice value of 30.

```
-------------------------
|   p_id    = 6         |
|   0<=p_cpu<=60        |
|   p_pri   = 60        |
|   p_nice = 20         |
|   p_link = 0          |
|                       |
-------------------------
Running Process


-------------------------       -------------------------       -------------------------
|   p_id    = 7         |       |   p_id    = 8         |       |   p_id    = 5         |
|   p_cpu  = 30         |       |   p_cpu = 15          |       |   p_cpu = 0           |
|   p_pri  = 75         |       |   p_pri = 67          |       |   p_pri  = 60         |
|   p_nice = 20         |       |   p_nice= 20          |       |   p_nice= 20          |
|   p_link = ---|-----> |       |   p_link=----|----->  |       |   p_link= 0           |
|                       |       |                       |       |                       |
-------------------------       -------------------------       -------------------------
  ^
  |
 runq
```

Fig. 2-10. Run queue and running process during third second.

```
-------------------       -------------------       -------------------       -------------------
|  p_id   = 6     |       |  p_id   = 7     |       |  p_id   = 8     |       |  p_id   = 5     |
|  p_cpu  = 30    |       |  p_cpu = 15     |       |  p_cpu = 7      |       |  p_cpu = 0      |
|  p_pri  = 75    |       |  p_pri = 67     |       |  p_pri = 63     |       |  p_pri = 60     |
|  p_nice = 20    |       |  p_nice= 20     |       |  p_nice= 20     |       |  p_nice= 20     |
|  p_link = ---|----> |   |  p_link=----|----> |    |  p_link=----|----> |    |  p_link= 0      |
|                 |       |                 |       |                 |       |                 |
-------------------       -------------------       -------------------       -------------------
 ^
 |
 runq
```

Fig. 2-11. Run queue after 3 seconds.

SLEEPING AND WAKING

When a process is unable to execute promptly for any number of reasons, that process will normally enter a state known as sleeping. For example, when a process makes an I/O request, it will issue some type of read call. Because I/O is a slow (relative to CPU speed) process, the requesting process will normally sleep. The sleeping is due to the fact that the process must wait for results. Rather than consume CPU resources by actively running and waiting, the process issues a sleep( ) system call and then relinquishes the CPU with

30

```
-------------------------
|    p_id    = 5    |
| O(=p_cpu(=60  |
|    p_pri   = 60   |
|    p_nice  = 20   |
|    p_link  = O    |
|                   |
-------------------------
```

Running Process

```
-------------------------      ----------------------      ----------------------
|    p_id    = 6   |           |   p_id    = 7   |         |   p_id    = 8   |
|    p_cpu   = 30  |           |   p_cpu   = 15  |         |   p_cpu   = 7   |
|    p_pri   = 75  |           |   p_pri   = 67  |         |   p_pri   = 63  |
|    p_nice  = 20  |           |   p_nice= 20    |         |   p_nice= 20    |
|    p_link  = ---|----->|     |   p_link=----|----->|     |   p_link= O     |
|                  |           |                 |         |                 |
-------------------------      ----------------------      ----------------------
```
```
^
|
runq
```

Fig. 2-12. Run queue and running process during fourth second.

```
------------------      --------------------      ------------------      -------------------
| p_id    = 5  |        | p_id    = 6  |          | p_id    = 7  |        | p_id    = 8  |
| p_cpu   = 30 |        | p_cpu   = 15 |          | p_cpu   = 7  |        | p_cpu   = 3  |
| p_pri   = 75 |        | p_pri   = 67 |          | p_pri   = 63 |        | p_pri   = 61 |
| p_nice  = 20 |        | p_nice= 20   |          | p_nice= 20   |        | p_nice= 20   |
| p_link  = ---|----->| | p_link=----|----->|     | p_link=----|----->|   | p_link= O    |
|              |        |              |          |              |        |              |
------------------      --------------------      ------------------      -------------------
```
```
^
|
runq
```

Fig. 2-13. Run queue after 4 seconds.

a swtch( ) call (note that not all processes will sleep and relinquish the CPU,
rather they will spin in a tight loop-polling for results—in this case a process
may be preempted and replaced on the run queue but does not ever go to sleep).

System calls are the primary cause of wait states resulting in a process
going to sleep. The majority of the waits are while:

☐ waiting for an I/O completion;
☐ waiting for a scarce but sharable resource such as an I/O channel;
☐ waiting for a non-sharable resource such as a locked file or record;
☐ waiting for a synchronization event.

```
-----------------------------
|   p_id    = 8  |
|  3<=p_cpu<=63  |
|   p_pri   = 61 |
|   p_nice = 20  |
|   p_link = 0   |
|                |
-----------------------------
```

Running Process

```
-----------------------------        -----------------------------        -----------------------------
|   p_id    = 5  |        |   p_id   = 6  |        |   p_id    = 7  |
|   p_cpu   = 30 |        |   p_cpu = 15  |        |   p_cpu   = 7  |
|   p_pri   = 75 |        |   p_pri = 67  |        |   p_pri   = 63 |
|   p_nice = 20  |        |   p_nice= 20  |        |   p_nice= 20  |
|   p_link = ---|----->|        |   p_link=----|----->|        |   p_link= 0   |
|                |        |               |        |               |
-----------------------------        -----------------------------        -----------------------------
```
```
^
|
runq
```

Fig. 2-14. Run queue and running process during fifth second.

```
-----------------        -----------------        -----------------        -----------------
|   p_id   = 8  |        |   p_id   = 5  |        |   p_id   = 6  |        |   p_id    = 7  |
|   p_cpu  = 31 |        |   p_cpu  = 15 |        |   p_cpu  = 7  |        |   p_cpu   = 3  |
|   p_pri  = 75 |        |   p_pri  = 67 |        |   p_pri  = 63 |        |   p_pri   = 61 |
|   p_nice = 20 |        |   p_nice= 20  |        |   p_nice= 20  |        |   p_nice= 20  |
|   p_link = ---|----->|        |   p_link=----|----->|        |   p_link=----|----->|        |   p_link= 0   |
|               |        |               |        |               |        |               |
-----------------        -----------------        -----------------        -----------------
```
```
^
|
runq
```

Fig. 2-15. Run queue after 5 seconds.

```
-----------------        -----------------        -----------------        -----------------
|   p_id   = 5  |        |   p_id   = 6  |        |   p_id   = 7  |        |   p_id   = 8  |
|   p_cpu  = 0  |        |   p_cpu  = 0  |        |   p_cpu  = 0  |        |   p_cpu  = 0  |
|   p_pri  = 60 |        |   p_pri  = 40 |        |   p_pri  = 70 |        |   p_pri  = 60 |
|   p_nice = 10 |        |   p_nice= 20  |        |   p_nice= 30  |        |   p_nice= 20  |
|   p_link = ---|----->|        |   p_link=----|----->|        |   p_link=----|----->|        |   p_link= 0   |
|               |        |               |        |               |        |               |
-----------------        -----------------        -----------------        -----------------
```
```
^
|
runq
```

Fig. 2-16. Run queue at start of example.

```
----------------------
!   p_id    = 6   !
! 0<=p_cpu<=60 !
!   p_pri   = 40 !
!   p_nice = 20 !
!   p_link = 0   !
!                    !
----------------------
```

Running Process

```
----------------------          ----------------------          ----------------------
!   p_id    = 5   !          !   p_id   = 7   !          !   p_id   = 8   !
!   p_cpu  = 0   !          !   p_cpu = 0   !          !   p_cpu = 0   !
!   p_pri   = 60 !          !   p_pri = 70 !          !   p_pri = 60 !
!   p_nice = 10 !          !   p_nice= 30 !          !   p_nice= 20 !
!   p_link = ---!---->!   p_link=----!---->!   p_link= 0   !
!                    !          !                    !          !                    !
----------------------          ----------------------          ----------------------
```
^
!
runq

Fig. 2-17. Run queue and running process.

```
----------------          ----------------          ----------------          ----------------
!  p_id   = 6 !          !  p_id   = 5 !          !  p_id   = 7 !          !  p_id   = 8 !
!  p_cpu  = 30 !          !  p_cpu = 0   !          !  p_cpu = 0   !          !  p_cpu = 0   !
!  p_pri   = 75 !          !  p_pri = 50 !          !  p_pri = 70 !          !  p_pri = 60 !
!  p_nice = 20 !          !  p_nice= 10 !          !  p_nice= 30 !          !  p_nice= 20 !
!  p_link = ---!---->!  p_link=----!---->!  p_link=----!---->!  p_link= 0   !
!                !          !                !          !                !          !                !
----------------          ----------------          ----------------          ----------------
```
^
!
runq

Fig. 2-18. Run queue after 1 second.

The fact of critical importance is that a sleeping process is not able to be run. Because it is not able to be run, it is not on the run queue, but exists on a sleep queue as will be seen.

When the event for which a process was waiting occurs, such as the completion of an I/O or the death of a child process, that process is awakened. The awakening of a process causes the process to be added to the current run queue to wait for swtch( ) to make it the running process. There is no specified length of time between the wake-up and the swtch( ) to running.

```
-----------------------
;   p_id    = 5   ;
;   O<=p_cpu<=60  ;
;   p_pri   = 50  ;
;   p_nice = 10   ;
;   p_link = O    ;
;                 ;
-----------------------
```

Running Process

```
-----------------------        -----------------------        -----------------------
;    p_id   = 6  ;              ;   p_id   = 7  ;              ;   p_id   = 8  ;
;    p_cpu  = 30 ;              ;   p_cpu = O   ;              ;   p_cpu = O   ;
;    p_pri  = 75 ;              ;   p_pri = 70  ;              ;   p_pri = 60 ;
;    p_nice = 20 ;              ;   p_nice= 30  ;              ;   p_nice= 20 ;
;    p_link = ---;---->;        ;   p_link=----;---->;         ;   p_link= O   ;
;                ;              ;               ;              ;               ;
-----------------------        -----------------------        -----------------------
^
;
runq
```

Fig. 2-19. Run queue and running process during second second.

```
-----------------          -----------------          -----------------          -----------------
;  p_id   = 5  ;            ;  p_id   = 6  ;            ;  p_id   = 7  ;            ;  p_id   = 8  ;
;  p_cpu  = 30 ;            ;  p_cpu = 7   ;            ;  p_cpu = O   ;            ;  p_cpu = O   ;
;  p_pri  = 65 ;            ;  p_pri = 63  ;            ;  p_pri = 70  ;            ;  p_pri = 60 ;
;  p_nice = 10 ;            ;  p_nice= 20  ;            ;  p_nice= 30  ;            ;  p_nice= 20 ;
;  p_link = ---;---->;      ;  p_link=----;---->;       ;  p_link=----;---->;       ;  p_link= O  ;
;              ;            ;              ;            ;              ;            ;             ;
-----------------          -----------------          -----------------          -----------------
^
;
runq
```

Fig. 2-20. Run queue after 2 seconds.

When a process goes to sleep, it is said to be *sleeping on an event*. The event on which a process is sleeping is the system process which must occur before the sleeping process can continue. Various types of events which can cause sleep waits have unique identifiers within the system. The exact identifiers of events are determined by the specific implementation of the operating system. The identifiers for events are referred to as channels and are stored in the process table entry, p__wchan.

Every event, and therefore each event identifier, has a *sleep queue* associated with it. The sleep queue is another logical view of the process table. Each sleep

```
-----------------------
|   p_id    = 8     |
| 0<=p_cpu<=60      |
|   p_pri   = 60    |
|   p_nice = 20     |
|   p_link = 0      |
|                   |
-----------------------
```

Running Process

```
-----------------------      -----------------------      -----------------------
|   p_id   = 5     |         |   p_id   = 6     |          |   p_id   = 7     |
|   p_cpu  = 30    |         |   p_cpu = 15     |          |   p_cpu = 0      |
|   p_pri  = 65    |         |   p_pri = 67     |          |   p_pri = 70     |
|   p_nice = 10    |         |   p_nice= 20     |          |   p_nice= 30     |
|   p_link = ---|----->|     |   p_link=----|----->|       |   p_link= 0      |
|                  |         |                  |          |                  |
-----------------------      -----------------------      -----------------------
```
```
^
|
runq
```

Fig. 2-21. Run queue and running process during third second.

```
-----------------      -----------------      -----------------      -----------------
|  p_id   = 8   |      |  p_id   = 5   |      |  p_id   = 6   |      |  p_id   = 7   |
|  p_cpu  = 30  |      |  p_cpu = 15   |      |  p_cpu = 7    |      |  p_cpu = 0    |
|  p_pri  = 75  |      |  p_pri = 57   |      |  p_pri = 63   |      |  p_pri = 70   |
|  p_nice = 20  |      |  p_nice= 10   |      |  p_nice= 20   |      |  p_nice= 30   |
|  p_link = ---|----->||  p_link=----|----->||  p_link=----|----->||  p_link= 0    |
|               |      |               |      |               |      |               |
-----------------      -----------------      -----------------      -----------------
```
```
^
|
runq
```

Fig. 2-22. Run queue after 3 seconds.

queue is a singly-linked list in which all processes are identified as sleeping and therefore not able to be run, and each sleep queue is associated with one and only one event.

Each event may have more than one process sleeping on it. For example, if several processes need to update a particular record in a database, and that record is locked, all processes waiting for the record to unlock will sleep on that event (the unlocking of the record). When the event occurs, all the processes waiting on that event will wake and be added to the run queue. As soon as they again encounter a wait state, they will again be added to a sleep queue.

```
  -------------------
  |   p_id    = 5   |
  |15<=p_cpu<=75    |
  |   p_pri   = 57  |
  |   p_nice = 10   |
  |   p_link = 0    |
  |                 |
  -------------------
```

Running Process

```
  -------------------        -------------------        -------------------
  |   p_id   = 8    |        |   p_id   = 6    |        |   p_id   = 7    |
  |   p_cpu  = 30   |        |   p_cpu = 7     |        |   p_cpu = 0     |
  |   p_pri  = 75   |        |   p_pri = 63    |        |   p_pri = 70    |
  |   p_nice = 20   |        |   p_nice= 20    |        |   p_nice= 30    |
  |   p_link = ---|----->|   p_link=----|----->|   p_link= 0     |
  |               |        |               |        |                 |
  -------------------        -------------------        -------------------
  ^
  |
  runq
```

Fig. 2-23. Run queue and running process during fourth second.

```
  -----------------    -----------------    -----------------    -----------------
  |  p_id   = 5   |    |  p_id  = 8    |    |  p_id  = 6    |    |  p_id  = 7    |
  |  p_cpu  = 37  |    |  p_cpu = 15   |    |  p_cpu = 3    |    |  p_cpu = 0    |
  |  p_pri  = 66  |    |  p_pri = 67   |    |  p_pri = 61   |    |  p_pri = 70   |
  |  p_nice = 10  |    |  p_nice= 20   |    |  p_nice= 20   |    |  p_nice= 30   |
  |  p_link = ---|---->|  p_link=----|---->|  p_link=----|---->|  p_link= 0    |
  |             |      |             |      |             |      |               |
  -----------------    -----------------    -----------------    -----------------
  ^
  |
  runq
```

Fig. 2-24. Run queue after 4 seconds.

```
  -------------------    -------------------    -------------------
  |                 |    |                 |    |                 |
  |  p_wchan = ev1|    |  p_wchan = ev1|    |  p_wchan = ev1|
  |                 |    |                 |    |                 |
  |  p_link-------|------->|  p_link-------|------->|  p_link = 0   |
  |               |    |               |    |                 |
  -------------------    -------------------    -------------------
  ^
  |
  ev1 queue
```

Fig. 2-25. Diagram of sleep queue for Event Identifier 1.

In general, active processes are in one of three conditions: running, in the run queue or in a sleep queue. Another entry in the process table identifies the status of the process. The p_stat field is set equal either to SRUN (meaning it is not waiting for an event), or equal to SSLEEP if the process is sleeping.

When a process is put to sleep, it has its priority reset. Because sleeping processes are often waiting to use system resources, such as I/O channels, their priority is set such that when the resource becomes available, they will run quickly and free that resource. Once the priority has been set to system priority (39 or less), the priority is not recomputed every second (although p_cpu is updated). Thus, once a process with system priority begins running, it is likely to continue running until completion. Only another system priority process of higher priority will interrupt the process. By setting the priority of sleeping processes to various system priority levels (depending on the event they are sleeping on), the system ensures the fair and fast use of critical or scarce system resources.

The actual call to sleep( ) is sleep(event,priority). When this call is issued for a running process, the process table entries for the status (p_stat) the event (p_wchan) and the process priority (p_pri) are reset as follows:

sleep(event,priority)

p_stat = SSLEEP
p_wchan = event
p_pri = priority

When swtch( ) is called, the process is added to the appropriate sleep queue.

Once the interrupt occurs, indicating that the desired event has occurred, the wakeup( ) call is issued. The actual call to wakeup( ) is wakeup(event). When the wakeup( ) call is issued, all events sleeping on a particular process are awakened. The p_wchan variable is cleared and the p_stat is set to able to be run.

wakeup(event)

p_stat = SRUN
p_wchan = event

Once the wakeup( ) call has occurred an important sequence of events takes place. A system variable called curpri is maintained, storing the priority of the currently running process. As a result of the wakeup( ) call, curpri is compared with p_pri for the awakened process and if p_pri is less than curpri (that is, the awakened process has a higher priority than the running process) a system flag called runrun is set on.

The runrun flag is reset in swtch( ) every time it occurs. Thus, when the flag is set, it means that a process of high priority has awakened during the running of the current process. When this flag is set it causes swtch( ) to be triggered each time the processor switches from system (kernel) to user mode.

In this event, the current process will be preempted, qswtch( ) will execute to add the current process to the run queue and the newly awakened process of high priority will begin execution.

In the event that at some time the swtch( ) routine finds no run type events, the processor enters an idle state. The curpri variable is set to PIDLE. The system issues an idle( ) call and waits for any interrupt. As soon as an interrupt occurs, the system tries again to start execution of a process.

Fair Share Scheduling

The scheduling process as described schedules each process independently. Scheduling occurs without regard to any relationships between the processes or the users of the processes. A modification to the kernel scheduling algorithms makes it possible to schedule processes as parts of groups. For example, under the normal scheduling algorithms, if a group or department buys forty percent of the time on a UNIX system, there is no effective way to ensure that the group will get that amount of time. All processes regardless of group ownership will be scheduled without allowing any special access to the one group.

The modifications providing the fair share scheduler controls distribution of CPU resources so that groups of related processes can get specified amounts of CPU resource. The key to the fair share scheduler is that it is simple to implement and does not alter the underlying concepts of CPU scheduling. Within a group processes are scheduled exactly as they would be without fair share scheduling.

The first modification required is the establishment of "fair share groups." These fair share groups are assigned fair share group priorities reflecting the amount of CPU resource they are to receive. All processes get an extra field in the user area which is a pointer to a fair share group CPU usage field and this field is shared by all processes in the fair share group. The updating of this fair share group CPU usage field in combination with the fair share group priority ensures that the groups get the requisite amount of CPU resource.

Real Time Processing

As has been said before, UNIX is a time sharing system. Real time processing requires the immediate response to specific external events. Processes must be scheduled to run within a specified time after an event has occurred. While certain processes may occur quickly in the UNIX environment, quick is not the same as real time. As it currently exists, UNIX scheduling is not appropriate for real time processing.

In the UNIX environment, there can be no real guarantees on when a process will be scheduled. While priorites can be manipulated, real time response cannot be ensured solely with priority adjustment. Making UNIX even less suited to real time processing is the inherent fact that kernel processes are not preemptible. By definition, kernel processes may not be preempted, thus making it impossible to guarantee execution of a process in a particular time frame.

The UNIX kernel must be modified to make real time processing possible. To date, no UNIX system has done this effectively.

OF INTEREST TO PROGRAMMERS

The features of this chapter that are of primary interest to programmers are the impact of the nice( ) call and the bias away from CPU-bound processes. These two areas have direct impact on the apparent execution speed of a process from the user perspective. They are also to some extent controllable by the programmer.

The programmer who is not a superuser can only have negative effect on the nice value (stored in p__nice). This means that it is possible to make it virtually impossible for certain processes to execute unless no other process needs to operate. Setting a high nice value is a step that should be exercised with caution, since it can be so detrimental to the performance of certain programs. On the other hand, when the programmer is in complete control of the application execution environment, judicious use of the nice value can result in assuring that critical programs run while non-critical programs wait.

The scheduling algorithm used in UNIX provides a substantial bias towards those programs which require system resources and must wait for those resources. The programmer who attempts to increase performance of a module by reducing its disk I/O to an absolute minimum may find no advantage given the scheduling algorithm based around p__cpu (the CPU versus elapsed time ratio). Thus, when performance is an issue, several short I/O requests can be just as effective for optimal use as attempting to attach the resource for a long period and then process the information with no additional scarce resource utilization. Also, since sleeping events have their priorites readjusted, the CPU-intensive operation will find itself constantly preempted in favor of the system resource-intensive operations.

Summary

The UNIX operating system uses round robin scheduling as opposed to straight line scheduling. It allows many processes to be simultaneously present in memory and then gives each of them fair amounts of time in which to operate.

The allocation of time to processes is based on the one second time quantum. Each process has a maximum of one second during which it can execute uninterrupted. Once the time quantum for a process has elapsed, the process is preempted and another process begins execution.

The preemption of a process results in the occurrence of a context switch. During a context switch a "snapshot" of the execution environment of the process being preempted is taken. When that process gets another chance to run memory is restored to the image in the snapshot.

The clock interrupt handler controls the counting of time during execution. The clock interrupt handler is called many times a second (depending on the specific hardware). It is the interrupt handler which indicates whether a time quantum has elapsed.

Processes get the opportunity to run based upon priority, with the highest priority process always running first. Process priorities are based upon several factors, but the most significant is the amount of CPU time versus the elapsed time in memory. UNIX is biased towards non-CPU intensive processes.

When a process is preempted, or while it is waiting for some slow event (such as disk I/O) it will sleep. A sleeping process resides in either primary or secondary storage waiting to be awakened by the occurrence of an event. An event which could wake a process would be the preemption of another process. When a process is preempted, all sleeping processes are awakened (by the clock interrupt handler sending a wake up signal) and the highest priority process gets to run.

It is possible to modify the scheduling process within the kernel to allow for special situations. Fair share scheduling, where process groups are given consideration, is one such example of straight-forward kernel modification. The fair share scheduling concept for UNIX has been fully designed.

Certain other types of scheduling remain very difficult in UNIX. Real time operations are not easy since it is difficult to keep a process from being preempted and it is difficult to guarantee the length of time which may elapse between process executions.

Points to Ponder

Is a one second time quantum the best approach to tracking process run time? How would you modify this quantum approach to make UNIX a more efficient timesharing system?

What changes would be required to make UNIX reasonable for real time processing? Could these changes be made within the basic philosophy and constraints of UNIX?

3

Memory Management Under UNIX

The UNIX operating system distinguishes between two types of memory: *primary memory* and *secondary memory*. Primary memory is the main memory; what we familiarly associate with RAM or core memory. Primary memory is the part of memory where the activity of the running system takes place. Secondary memory is also known as the *swap device*. It is the area where memory images which are not currently being used are stored. The swap device or secondary memory may be a specially reserved portion of a disk device or even a tape.

Processes can only run if they have a *swapping image* in primary memory. The swapping image of a process is in essence its process image, but it is more specifically the portion of the process needed only when the process is running. For example, a process's process table entry is not part of the swapping image, because that information is necessary for scheduling even when the particular process is not running. The swapping image does include the code and data for a non-shared text process, the user stack, and the system stack.

Figure 3-1 shows two types of swapping images. When a more urgent or higher priority process requires immediate run-time, these are the swapping images that may be temporarily removed from primary memory and placed in secondary memory, allowing the more urgent or more active processes access to primary memory. In general, the swapping images stored on secondary memory will take longer to access than those in primary memory.

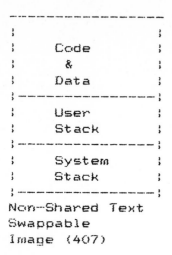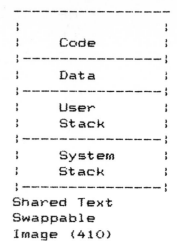

```
---------------------------              ----------------------------
;                       ;                ;                          ;
;       Code            ;                ;          Code            ;
;        &              ;                ;--------------------------;
;       Data            ;                ;          Data            ;
;-----------------------;                ;--------------------------;
;       User            ;                ;          User            ;
;       Stack           ;                ;          Stack           ;
;-----------------------;                ;--------------------------;
;       System          ;                ;          System          ;
;       Stack           ;                ;          Stack           ;
;-----------------------;                ;--------------------------;
    Non-Shared Text                          Shared Text
    Swappable                                Swappable
    Image (407)                              Image (410)
```

Fig. 3-1. Swapping Images.

The function swtch( ) has as its target the user area—that is, swtch( ) modifies the user area status and contents. When this function is invoked, the user area is placed on either the run queue, the sleep queue or is given running status. Thus, the function swtch( ) moves and reallocates the user area. In a very similar manner, swapping images are moved and reallocated by the swapper. The swapper is run as a process called sched( ). This process has as its task the manipulation of swapping images.

When discussing the swapper, a distinction must be drawn between non-shared text and shared text images and processes. The swapper can handle a non-shared text swapping image in a very straight-forward manner: the entire image can be swapped as needed. Swapping of shared text images and processes is somewhat more complex.

The code portion of a shared-text process may be used by more than one process at a time. Swapping out the code portion of the shared-text process with the rest of the process would be cumbersome at best and destructive at worst. A logical rectification of this problem is that swapping of the shared-text process must occur independently of the rest of the swapping process image.

A *text table* exists to track these shared-text processes. For each such process there is an entry in the text table. One member of this entry is the variable *x.ccount*. The x.ccount variable maintains a count of the number of processes in primary memory which are currently using the particular text portion. The text portion is swapped to secondary memory only when x.ccount is zero, showing that none of the processes in primary memory are using the particular text portion being counted.

WHY SWAP?

Why should swapping ever be necessary? Remember that UNIX is a multi-user, multi-process timesharing operating system. This operating system must function in a wide range of user environments. One feature of these environments which will vary widely is the amount of available memory. A certain minimal amount of memory is necessary. Beyond that minimum, there are no constraints on the necessary amount of available memory—although more memory is in many ways better, just as in any financial budget a certain amount of money is the minimum necessary to fund the endeavor, but more money is always welcome.

Suppose a particular system has one megabyte of memory available. Suppose also that this system has fifteen users, each working actively. As Fig. 3-2 shows, it doesn't take much imagination to see how that one megabyte of memory could be quickly consumed.

It would appear to be impossible to have all of these processes active simultaneously, but UNIX gives the impression of doing just that.

In the previous chapter we saw how UNIX scheduled processes to run so that they received fair amounts of time and system resource allocation. We also saw how some processes would sleep while waiting for resources. The swapper takes a process out of active (or primary memory) and places it on the swap device in order to make room for another process to run.

So that the users will be less likely to notice, sleeping processes are swapped out first, followed by processes of lower priority. By making use of the swap device, UNIX can juggle 1,014,000 bytes of processes in 1,000,000 bytes of memory (or even more processes or less memory) with minimal inconvenience to the user. Without swapping, a process could not be started or loaded until enough of the currently running processes had finished to make room for it in memory. While this would work, it could make it very difficult to start new processes on a busy system.

	Addresses	Size
0	0	n
1	First	Size
2	.	.
.	.	.
.	.	.
n	Last	0

Fig. 3-2. Sample system usage.

THE PRIMARY SWAPPER

The first process created when UNIX starts up is sched( ). This process has process I.D. 1 and is the swapper. It is always in system mode and has the highest priority. The most important aspect of the status of sched( ) is that it can never be preempted or swapped out itself. When it has no work to do it will sleep.

The task of the primary swapper is to swap processes into primary memory. When the swapper needs to make space in primary memory, it will swap processes into secondary memory as a temporary measure only to achieve its goal of swapping processes into main memory. When the swapper is activated, it will swap as many processes as it can into main memory.

The status of any process in memory is tracked by a flag in the process table. The nature of a flag is such that each of its bits has a meaning depending on whether or not that particular bit is turned on or off. The memory flag is called *p_flag*. Three bits of this flag are of particular interest, and are illustrated in Fig. 3-3.

When the SLOAD bit is set on, the process has its swapping image loaded in main memory and could be a candidate for swapping out. The SSYS bit, when turned on, indicates a process that may not be swapped out for any reason. The SSYS bit of sched( ) is always turned on so that the swapper may not be swapped out. When the SLOCK bit is on, that process has a physical I/O in progress and so may not be swapped out at this time, although it might become a candidate for swapping out at a later point.

As a slight digression, the usefulness of this particular bit should be becoming clear. Physical I/O consumes scarce resources. Control must be returned to the initiating process to release the I/O channel or device. If the process has been swapped out while waiting for I/O to be completed, it will take a long time to free the I/O device and thus slow down the other processes. By keeping the process in main memory, the I/O can be quickly completed.

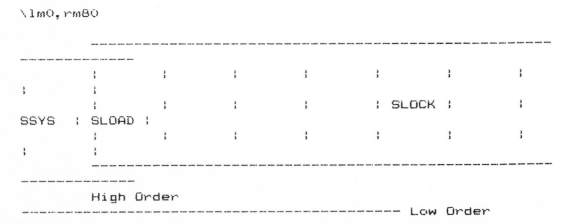

Fig. 3-3. Memory status maintained in p-flag.

Another entry in the process table is the key factor in determining whether or not a process will be swapped in or swapped out. The *p_time* field keeps track of how long the process has been in primary or secondary memory. The determination of whether it is counting primary or secondary time is based on the SLOAD bit. If SLOAD is on, then primary time is being counted. If SLOAD is off, secondary time is counted. Only the time a process is able to be run is counted if that process is on a secondary device. Thus a sleeping process in secondary memory does not increment *p_time*.

The p_time entry is another field which is updated once a second by the clock routine. Occasionally, the operating system adjusts p_time for certain processes beyond the standard one time a second update. This is done so that processes which are important to system execution are more difficult to swap out. Whenever a process is swapped, p_time is reset to zero. With some modifications, those processes which have the highest p_time values are most likely to be swapped.

Swapping Out

Processes are swapped out of main memory when additional space is needed in main memory. There are four types of events which can result in processes being swapped out:

☐ When the fork( ) call needs to allocate space for a child process;
☐ When a brk( ) call increases the process size;
☐ When a process stack grows beyond its initially allocated size;
☐ When the kernel needs space to swap in a process which had been previously swapped out.

The case where fork( ) causes swapping is of particular interest. It is the only instance where core memory is not relinquished on the swap out. The child, which fork( ) is creating, immediately gains control of the memory being freed so it never becomes generally available.

SWAPPING IN

The swapper has a subroutine known as swapin( ) which determines which processes to swap into main memory. The swapper's primary duty is to swap in as many processes as it can. The one rule that the swapper, through the use of swapin( ), strictly adheres to is that only processes that can run can be swapped in. Thus, a process sleeping in secondary memory will never be swapped in.

What happens when no processes are available for swapping in? The swapper goes to sleep. As was noted in the previous chapter, processes sleep on events and the swapper is no exception. Before the swapper sleeps, it sets a system flag called *runout*. The runout flag becomes the event identifier on which sched( ) is sleeping. Whenever *wakeup( )* is executed, processes on the particular wake-up channel are awakened and runout is cleared. Clearing runout causes a wakeup or runout which wakes the swapper. If some of the newly awakened processes are eligible for swapping, the swapper tries to swap them into main memory.

Once the swapper is set to swap in processes, what happens if not enough memory is available to allow the swapping in to occur? First, the swapper will try to swap a process out of main memory and into secondary memory. Sleeping processes are the most likely to be swapped. For a sleeping process to be swapped out the following formula must be satisfied:

$$p\_time + (p\_pri - PZERO)\ 0$$

where p_time is the time that the process has been in main memory, p_pri is the priority of the process, and PZERO is the boundary between high and low system priorities(40). Thus, user processes and low system priority processes will always be eligible for swapping out, while high system priority processes will need to have been in main memory for a long time before they become eligible.

Once all processes satisfying this condition have been found, the swapper will select the process which has the greatest sum of p_pri + p_time and only that process will be swapped out. If still more memory is required, the process is repeated.

If there are no more sleeping processes and still more memory is required, the swapper will consider swapping out processes that can run. A system flag called *outage* keeps track of the greatest length of time an executable process has been on the swap device. If outage is greater than 2 (the process has been on the swap device for greater than two seconds) then swapping out an executable process will be considered. The process swapped from main into secondary memory will be the process which produces the greatest value from the equation

$$p\_time + (p\_nice - NZERO) = 2$$

It is interesting to note that processes with high nice values are greatly penalized under UNIX. Not only will they have lower priorities and therefore get less run time, they are also more likely to end up on the swap device.

If not enough memory can be freed to allow the swapping in of an eligible process, even after trying to swap out both sleeping and executable processes, then the swapper will set a flag called *runin* and sleep on that event. The runin flag will be reset once a second, or whenever a process goes to sleep with a low system priority or lower priorities such as user priorities, or after any I/O completion. The resetting of runin will cause the swapper to wake and try again to load as many processes into main memory as it can.

THE AUXILIARY SWAPPER

The main purpose of the swapper is to move processes into main memory. It will swap processes out but only so that more processes may be swapped in. It is entirely possible that a process may want to swap itself out to the swap device. The two prime instances of this are when a process needs memory expansion to operate (generally the result of an sbrk( ) call); or when a process is forking a child process. Voluntary swap outs are handled by a process called *xsched( )*, the auxiliary swapper. This process only swaps processes out; xsched( ) never swaps processes in. However, xsched( ) is able to activate sched( ) when processes need to be swapped in.

As processes prepare to be swapped out voluntarily, they join a swap queue. Swap queues are almost identical to sleep and run queues. They are singly-linked lists. When the auxiliary swapper runs, it swaps all the processes on the swap queue into secondary memory. The auxiliary swapper sleeps while it is waiting for work or waiting for an I/O to complete. As soon as it wakes up, it swaps out all the processes on the swap queue.

MEMORY MANAGEMENT

For all of the complexities of choosing which processes are loaded in the main memory and which are loaded into secondary memory, the actual process of finding the appropriate location in memory is relatively simple. All memory is managed using a *first-fit* algorithm. This means that processes and data are loaded into memory at the first location where they fit. Even if the location is not the optimal size, as long as it is large enough, it is used.

Two memory maps are maintained. The memory map for the main memory is referred to as coremap. The memory map for secondary memory is called swapmap. Both maps are organized in the same way.

Memory maps are simple tables which contain information about free memory blocks. Each entry in the table contains an address and a size. The address refers to the location of some free space and the size tells how much free space is available at that location. The table is always maintained so that addresses are in numerical order, with low addresses at the top and high addresses at the bottom.

Figure 3-4 reflects a sample memory map. The first entry in a memory map always indicates the number of entries in the table. The entry with size 0 indicates the logical end of the memory map.

A malloc( ) call is a request for memory. When x bytes of memory are requested, the memory map is scanned for the first address pointing to free blocks of x bytes or greater. When such an address is found, the address is removed from the memory map. If the amount of free space at that address is greater than requested, then the remaining memory is returned to the map with the address adjusted to reflect the consumed memory.

The mfree( ) works in reverse. Its job is to deallocate memory. This call updates the map to reflect that the amount of memory returned is now available at the specified address. If addresses can be combined to form single large pieces of memory, this is done at the time of the mfree( ) call.

```
User      PID      Process Executable Image Size

a         34       25000
          56       76000
b         21       121000
c         33       45000
          32       43000
d         101      100000
e         87       75000
f         65       33000
g         55       12000
h         78       48000
i         51       56000
j         52       135000
k         57       13000
l         29       23000
m         28       98000
n         37       75000
o         71       36000
                   --------
Total              1014000 bytes
```

Fig. 3-4. Sample memory map.

DEMAND PAGING

A word needs to be said about *demand paging*. While the approach to process swapping described in this chapter reflects moving the entire process into or out of main memory, there is an alternative approach. UNIX V, depending on the hardware architecture, can support a swapping technique known as demand paging. This technique divides the code and data of the swapping image into pages. Pages are the smallest unit of memory referred to with respect to hardware protection. When demand paging is used, instead of the entire process being swapped in or out, only pages (or parts) of a process are swapped in or out. This approach allows for the swapping of much smaller units, which can greatly improve the efficiency of the system. Conceptually, demand paging follows the same rules as full process swapping, with the difference that somewhat more complex structures are necessary to track the precise pages which or may not be swapped at a particular time.

Demand paging has two hardware and architectural requirements. First, it requires that the memory architecture be based on pages. Second, it requires that the CPU have restartable instructions. When paging is permissible it allows the process to be broken into sections called pages. When main memory is required, or when a process is loaded, only pages (or portions) of the process are loaded. It is these pages which are swapped between main memory and the swap device. The real benefit of demand paging is that more processes can be loaded and active in main memory and processes which would not be executable due to their size may be run in a paging environment. A process of 4 to 5 megabytes can be run in less than 1 megabyte of memory in a system supporting paging. With these benefits, paging is transparent to the user programs—reprogramming to fit paging is not necessary.

When paging is being used, several pages of a program are in main memory at a time. These pages in main memory are referred to as the working set. When a process is running, various pages are being used. If the page required is not in active memory a page fault occurs. The ultimate resolution of a page fault is the addition of the required page to the working set.

OF INTEREST TO PROGRAMMERS

Memory management is an area of UNIX that is particularly relevant to the job that the programmer does. The first feature of memory management of interest to programmers is the difference in treatment of shared text and non-shared text code. Since the code portion of shared-text processes tends to remain in main memory, it is much more efficient to use the shared-text model for program development. Only the data and stack need to be swapped after the first load, and other processes are able to share the code. Shared text is the default model under UNIX V, so it should be used in all cases except when the code must be self-modifying.

It is possible to set processes so that they will never be swapped out of memory. Setting a process for no swap means turning on the SSYS bit of p__flag. This is accomplished by using the stickybit of the privilege codes in the inode of a file. The stickybit can be set with the chmod command. Keep in mind, however, that once a process is locked into main memory, that portion of main memory can never be reused. If the amount of main memory available for swapping in is reduced to too low a level, the other processes may get very little run time as they spend all their time in the swapping process.

Notice that there is a heavy bias toward I/O. Processes completing I/O are locked into memory. If the system can be balanced so that some processes require intensive I/O while others are less I/O-bound, the system performance will be much better overall than in the case where all or most processes are either I/O- or CPU-bound.

Adjusting the nice value for a process to allow other processes more run time can be a major disadvantage. The p__nice variable is the major factor in swapping out an executable process. Be certain that a process is really of a very low priority before adjusting its nice value.

The memory management algorithm tends to leave the large portions of free space at high memory. This fact can be used to a programmer's advantage in certain cases where specific memory locations are requested. Keep in mind that if enough memory is not available for a malloc( ) request, the return will be a null. This value should always be tested for before trying to use the memory. Failure to do so will certainly result in the corruption of critical memory locations.

Summary

The ability of UNIX to manage and maintain its memory in an efficient and clean manner is key to its performance as a timesharing operating system. UNIX divides memory into two (or more) segments. The traditional part of memory from which processes run is known as main memory. When main memory is fully occupied, processes and data are stored on secondary memory devices. These secondary memory devices may be portions of core allocated as secondary memory, or they may be disk, tape or other similar storage devices.

The swapping image of a process is that portion of a process image which is required only when the process is executing. For a process to be executing it must be in primary memory. When a process is to be moved into or out of main memory, or go from executing to non-executing status, two system functions control what happens. The swtch( ) call causes the user area to be modified to reflect the new process status. The swapper, known as sched( ) moves the swapping image to the appropriate memory location. The swapper always tries to swap images into memory, it only swaps out when there is insufficient main memory. When a process requests a voluntary swap out, the xsched( ) call (the auxiliary swapper) handles the swapping out function.

All memory, both primary and secondary is handled on a first fit basis. There is no attempt made to optimize memory usage. As soon as memory sufficient to the task is located, it is used even though it may cause memory fragmentation. The free memory is tracked via two memory maps—one for primary memory and one for secondary memory. These maps simply contain the starting address and number of blocks of free memory.

Demand paging, which has long been a feature of BSD UNIX has been incorporated into ATT UNIX System V. Demand paging allows portions of processes known as pages to be swapped in and out of memory instead of entire process images. This allows processes which are larger than available memory to execute and makes memory use more efficient.

Points to Ponder

Devise an algorithm to optimize memory utilization. In other words, design an approach in which UNIX would use a best fit rather than a first fit technique. What are the advantages and disadvantages of such a technique?

4

Interprocess Communications

One of the most interesting things about processes in a UNIX environment is that they are entirely self-contained. Processes use only their own data areas and are totally independent of the execution of processes around them. While this makes the handling of individual processes much less complex, it raises questions about how to handle the passing of information between processes.

Why would information need to be passed between processes? If two processes use the same data file or even the same terminal each must know when that file or terminal is available. In the case of piping, the results of one process must be made available for processing by another process. It is often the case that one process must complete execution or a portion of execution before another process can continue. All of these examples are handled by the interprocess communications facilities available under UNIX.

The UNIX interprocess communications facilities allow processes to exchange information. These facilities also permit the synchronization of processes. *Process synchronization* is the controlling of the timing of two or more processes so that the execution of various activities occurs at meaningful times in the life of the other process or processes.

Seven distinct mechanisms are provided for interprocess communication. Most interprocess communications convey information while they aid in synchronization. Nevertheless, each of the types of interprocess communication tends to be more useful in either information exchange or in synchronization. The various mechanisms and their primary functionality are listed and briefly described in Fig. 4-1.

Messages	Packets of data sent by one process and selectively received by another.
Shared memory	Common data areas used by more than one process.
Pipes	Special types of data files which make data available on a first-in, first-out (FIFO) basis.
Process Tracing	Information exchange and process control between a parent and child process, primarily used in debugging.
Synchronization Signals	System flags indicating the occurrance of specific events.
Semaphores	Definable flags indicating the occurrence of specific events.
Death Of Child	Special instance of signal telling parent that child has completed execution.

Fig. 4-1. Seven mechanisms for Interprocess Communication.

There are also system calls available to programmers that allow programmable control of interprocess communications. These system calls are listed and briefly defined in Fig. 4-2, and will be fully presented in the "Of Interest to Programmers" section of this chapter. Reference to these calls will be made throughout the chapter.

SIGNALS

Perhaps the most commonly referred to interprocess communications facility in UNIX is that of signals. Signals are most commonly used to communicate the occurrence of a specific event between related processes. Figure 4-3 shows the various signals which can be sent.

Signals are posted by one process and received by another or the same process. The receiving process performs an action appropriate to the signal received.

Interprocess Communication Facility	System Call	Description
Signal	signal()	Specifies what to do when signal is received.
	kill()	Sends a signal to a process or group of processes.
	pause()	Suspend the process until receipt of the signal.
Pipes	pipe()	Creates an interprocess channel.
	mknod()	Make a file, in this case, the file is to be FIFO.
Wait For Child	wait()	Wait for child process to stop or terminate.
	exit()	Terminate process.
Process Tracing	ptrace()	Trace a process.
Messages	msgget()	Get a message queue.
	msgsnd()	Send a message to a message queue.
	msgrcv()	Read a message from a message queue.
	msgctl()	Perform a message control operation.
Semaphores	semget()	Get a set of semaphores.
	semop()	Perform semaphore operations.
	semctl()	Perform a semaphore control operation.

Fig. 4-2. Interprocess Communication system calls.

Shared Memory	shmget()	Get a shared memory segment.
	shmat()	Attach the specified shared memory segment.
	shmdt()	Detach the specified shared memory segment.
	shmctl()	Perform shared memory control operation.

Fig. 4-2. Continued.

As was mentioned previously, signals are most commonly used between related processes. In general the processes will be related in one of three ways. The processes will either have the same effective user I.D., they will all be being controlled by the same terminal, or they will have a parent/child relationship.

The kill( ) system call sends SIGKILL (09) to processes with the same effective user I.D. with the provision that only the owner of a process or the superuser can kill a process. The SIGINT(02) and SIGQUIT(03) signals are

Value	Type	Description
01	SIGHUP	hangup
02	SIGINT	interupt
03	SIGQUIT	quit
04	SIGILL	illegal instruction
05	SIGTRAP	trace trap
06	SIGIOT	IOT instruction
07	SIGEMT	EMT instruction
08	SIGFPT	floating point exception
09	SIGKILL	kill
10	SIGBUS	bus error
11	SIGSEGV	segmentation violation
12	SIGSYS	bas argument to system call
13	SIGPIPE	write on pipe with no one to read it
14	SIGALRM	alarm clock
15	SIGTERM	software termination
16	SIGUSR1	user defined signal 1
17	SIGUSR2	user defined signal 2
18	SIGCLD	death of a child
19	SIGPWR	power failure

Fig. 4-3. UNIX signals.

54

sent to processes sharing the same terminal. The death of a child notification signal, SIGCLD(18), is sent to the parent of the process which, by definition, will have the same effective user I.D. A system call error signal, SIGSYS(12), is sent from a process to itself. A trap signal, SIGTRAP(05), is sent from a process to itself. These examples illustrate the simple fact that signals sent between unrelated processes are uncommon indeed.

When a process posts a signal, it updates a field in the process table for the process to which the signal is being sent. The p_sig field in the process table is a flag with each bit indicating the status of a signal for the process. Since signals are maintained by a single bit, an important consequence is that signals cannot be queued. When a signal is sent to a process, a single bit is turned on in the process table. If the signal is sent again before the process handles the bit, the bit remains on.

When the process does finally handle the bit, the bit remains on, no matter how many times the signal was sent. Repeated sending of the signal does not alter the bit-on or bit-off status. There is no memory of the receipt of multiple occurrences of the same signal.

Signals can only be processed when a process is running, and the processing of signals always occurs in system mode. Thus, a signal will be processed just after a process wakes up to run, or whenever the process is preparing to return from a system call.

While the range of signals which may be sent is limited, the action taken when a signal is received can be varied. In the user area for a process there is a table called *u_signal*. The u_signal table has twenty entries, each representing the action to be taken for each of the signals which can be received. There are three possible actions which can be taken for each signal received: the default action (SIG_DFL) which has a value of 0 causes a process to terminate; the ignore action (SIG_IGN) which has a value of any odd integer causes the signal to be ignored; any non-zero even value is taken as the address of a function to be executed upon the receipt of that signal. Note that the kill signal may not be caught to cause the execution of another process. The signal( ) system call allows the entries in u_signal to be changed.

When the time comes for a process to handle its signals, two internal functions are used. The issig( ) function checks for the existence of any non-ignore action signals for the particular process. If there are signals which require processing, the psig( ) function carries out the appropriate action beginning with the lowest posted signal.

It should be noted that the death of a child is simply a case of a signal being sent. While the death of a child is often referred to and considered some special type of interprocess communication, it is in actuality simply the posting of signal SIGCLD(18) to the parent process.

PROCESS TRACING

Process tracing is a fairly primitive form of interprocess communication, particularly useful in the case of debugging. The essence of process tracing is a sleep-wake relationship between a controlling and a controlled process (always a parent and a child).

A process (generally a debugger like sdb) will spawn a child process to be traced. It will control the process spawned with the ptrace( ) system call. The ptrace( ) system call uses signals to switch back and forth between the tracing process (the parent) and the traced process (the child).

PIPES

There are two types of pipes, named and unnamed. The pipe( ) system call is used to create and initiate unnamed pipes. The mknod( ) system call is used to create a file of first-in, first-out (FIFO) type. All pipes are simply FIFO files written to by one process or set of processes and read by another process or set of processes. Only related processes can share unnamed pipes, while unrelated processes can share only named pipes.

The basic function of a pipe is to allow process data to be written into one end of the pipe or pipeline, and read out of the other end. With this relationship in mind, we can see that there are four conditions which can occur:

☐ A successful write into a pipeline;
☐ A successful read from a pipeline;
☐ An unsuccessful write to a pipeline because the pipe is full;
☐ An unsuccessful read from a pipeline because the pipe is empty.

The first two of these conditions are normal pipe reads and writes and result in normal process functioning. The second two conditions result in process synchronization. In the last two cases, the process reading or writing will sleep until the read or write can be successfully completed. The processes are automatically synchronized with respect to other pipe reading and writing activities.

SEMAPHORES, MESSAGES, AND SHARED MEMORY

The triad of interprocess communication facilities—semaphores, messages, and shared memory—have a common control and usage command structure. For the purposes of this chapter, the first three characters of the commands for these facilities will be fff. The fff can be replaced by sem when dealing specifically with the semaphore commands, by mes when dealing with the message commands, and shm when dealing with the shared memory commands.

The fffget( ) system call uses a key to create or to access the appropriate structure for the interprocess communications facility. When the system call is issued with the appropriate key, an identifier is assigned and an appropriate structure is created or assigned. The structure for a facility contains permissions for the various operations which may be performed, as well as information specific to the facility.

The structure created or assigned by fffget( ) is given an identifier. The assigned identifier is derived from a system table maintained for each of these facilities. There is one system table for each of the interprocess communications facilities. The *facility identifier* is a unique nonnegative integer.

The fffctl( ) system call invokes various operating system routines to handle facility requests. In general, the fffctl( ) system call is used to get facility status information and to set facility control values. In the case of semaphores, the semctl( ) system call can initialize the value of a semaphore.

The fffop( ) system calls perform facility-specific operations.

The creator of one of these interprocess communication facility structures is the owner (based on effective user I.D.). Only the owner or superuser can change the ownership of an interprocess communication facility structure. Operation permissions for these facilities are contained in a nine-bit field. The first three bits of the field reflect owner permissions, the second three bits reflect group permissions and the last three bits reflect other permissions. The first bit of each group of three indicates read permission, the second bit reflects write permission, and the third bit is not used.

SEMAPHORES

Semaphores are an interprocess communications facility used to implement a wait and signal mechanism similar in many ways to sleep( ) and wakeup( ). In fact, the semaphore calls actually use sleep( ) and wakeup( ) to implement this facility. A semaphore is really just a numeric value. Depending on the particular numeric value certain processes will wake. A *semaphore* set may contain more than one semaphore, but any operations performed on the set are performed on all semaphores within the set. There is an optional undo operation for semaphores, which, when a process terminates, reverses all operations performed on a semaphore set by that process.

Semaphore structures, which contain semaphore information for a semaphore set, are allocated, deallocated and managed just like memory. A table equivalent to coremap and swapmap called semmap maintains the pool of available semaphore structures. Semaphore set allocation is performed with semget( ).

A semaphore structure contains four fields. It contains a field called *semval( )* which contains the current value of a semaphore. The field *sempid( )* contains the process I.D. of the last process that operated on the semaphore. The number of processes waiting for semval( ) to be greater than its current value is stored in *semncnt( )*. Finally, *semzcnt( )* contains the number of processes waiting for semval to be zero.

The semctl( ) system call sets or gets the value of the semvals in a semaphore set. All semvals will be set to the value specified by semctl( ). Thus, even though there may be multiple semaphores in a set, all will have the same value at all times.

The semop( ) system call causes the values of the semvals depending on the value of the operator specified (in sem__op) and the current value of sem__op. All processes will stop if sem__op is less than zero and semval is less than the absolute value of sem__op or if sem__op is equal to zero and semval not equal to zero. If sem__op is greater than zero, it is added to semval at which time all processes waiting for semval to attain a specific value will wakeup, check to see if semval now contains the correct value and if not will go back to sleep. Thus process operation is controlled by the value of sem_op in the semop( ) system call.

MESSAGES

In interprocess communications, messages are used with two commands. These commands are send a message (the *msgsnd( )* system call) and receive a message (the *msgrcv( )* system call). The message sender specifies a message type along with the message text. The message receiver uses the message type as a selection criterion. If a message type of zero is chosen as the selection criterion, then the receiver selects the messages chronologically. If the receiver cannot find a message of the type desired, it can sleep( ) until the proper type is sent to it. It is therefore possible to use messages for synchronization of processes.

Messages are blocks of text stored in structures along with the message type. The length of the text can be defined by the user. The buffers containing the *message structures* are pointed to *message queue headers*. The message queue is a singly linked list of headers. The space required for the message structures is managed just as memory is managed—using a msgmap( ) table and performing malloc( ) and mfree( ) to get the necessary space.

When a message is sent the following steps must be performed. First, a free message queue header must be allocated. Second, space for the message itself must be allocated. The message area and the header must be filled with the pertinent message information. Finally, the newly created message queue header must be linked to the message queue.

Receiving a message can be done either by message type or by chronological order (first-in, first-out). Once the message is received, the header is unlinked, the message space is deallocated and the message queue header is freed.

A process using the message facility will sleep when one of two conditions occurs. Processes will sleep either when trying to read from an empty queue or trying to write to a full queue. Thus, in addition to conveying information, the message facility will perform process synchronization as necessary.

SHARED MEMORY

The shared memory interprocess communication facility is by far the fastest of the facilities. *Shared memory* is precisely what it sounds like: it allows processes to read from and write to a common area of memory. This common area is linked within the data space for the processes.

When the shmget( ) system call is issued a physical shared-memory segment is allocated and a shared memory identifier is returned. The shared memory identifier is used by all processes using the shared memory facility.

The shmat( ) system call does not allocate memory. Instead it attaches memory to an already existing shared memory segment. It then maps that virtual shared memory segment into an already allocated memory segment.

If no virtual address is specified, then the first available address following the data segment is used. Caution must be taken in specifying the address of shared memory so that the stack does not grow up into the space. Permission is read-only or read-write for a process, determined on a per process basis.

Various processes may use the shared memory segment during its existence. As a process finishes, it issues the shmdt( ) system call to detach from the shared memory space. After the last process using the shared memory segment has detached from it, the segment is physically removed.

OF INTEREST TO PROGRAMMERS

Two major issues regarding interprocess communications are of interest to programmers: which facility to use and how to use the various facilities.

For communications to facilitate debugging, the process tracing facility should be used. For synchronization, either signals or semaphores should be used. Signals should be used when certain responses are required for the limited number of signals which can be sent. When a process should sleep or wake depending on the occurrence and a wide range of user defined events, semaphores should be used. When more information than simply the occurrence of an event must be conveyed, either messages, shared memory or pipes should be used. Messages should be used for transferring data packets of unknown length but of classifiable type. Pipes should be used for fixed length, single type information. Shared memory should be used for the high speed transfer of limited amounts of information among several processes.

All the interprocess communication facilities are controlled by system calls. The rest of this chapter lists the system calls with their parameters, include files and function.

```
/* signal()-specify what to do upon receipt of a signal */

#include signal.h

int       sig;      /* the signal type */

int       (*func)();         /* pointer to function to execute

                       on receipt of signal */

int       (*signal (sig,func))()


/* kill()-send a signal to a process or a group of processes*/

#include signal.h

int       pid,      /* if pid0, signal sent to pid;

                       if pid==0, signal sent to all processes;
```

```
                         if pid==(-1) and user I.D. of sender is not

                             super user, signal sent to all processes

                             with same user id;

                         if pid==(-1) and user I.D. of sender is super

                             user, signal sent to all processes;

                         if pid(-1), signal will be sent to all

                             processes whose process group I.D. is equal

                             to the absolute value of pid */

         sig;      /* signal to be sent */

   int       kill(pid,sig);



   /* pause()-suspend process until signal */

   int       pause();



   /* wait()-wait for child process to stop or terminate */

   int       *stat_loc;       /* status of child process */

   int       wait(stat_loc);



   /* exit()-terminate process */

   int       status;          /* status of terminated process */

   int       exit(status)



   /* pipe()-create an interprocess channel */

   int       fildes[2];       /* fildes[0]-file descriptor opened

                                 for reading;

                                 fildes[1]-file descriptor opened

                                 for writing */
```

```
int     pipe(fildes)


/* ptrace()-process trace */

int     request,        /* action to be taken by ptrace */

        pid,            /* process I.D. of child */

        addr,           /* address of word in chaild data area */

        data;           /* address of value to be written */

int     ptrace(request,pid,addr,data)


/* msgget()-get message queue */

#include sys\types.h

#inlcude sys\ipc.h

#include sys\msg.h

key_t   key;            /* key for message queue */

int     msgflg:         /* message status *.

int     msgget(key,msgflg)


/* msgctl()-message control operations */

#include sys\types.h

#include sys\ipc.h

#include sys\msg.h

int     msqid,          /* message queue identifier */

        cmd;            /* control operation */

struct  msqid_ds *buf;  /* message data structure */

int     msgctl(msqid,cmd,buf)


/* msgop-message operations */
```

```
/* msgsnd()-send message */

#include sys\types.h

#include sys\ipc.h

#include sys\msg.h

int      msqid;            /* message queue identifier */

struct   msgbuf *msgp;     /* structure containing message and type */

int      msgsz;            /* length of message text */

int      msgflg;           /* message status */

int      msgsnd(msqid,msgp,msgsz,msgflg)


/* msgrcv()-receive message */

#include sys\types.h

#include sys\ipc.h

#include sys\msg.h

int      msqid;            /* message queue identifier */

struct   msgbuf *msgp;     /* structure to contain message */

int      msgsz;            /* length of message text */

long     msgtyp;           /* message type */

int      msgflg;           /* message status */

int      msgsnd(msqid,msgp,msgsz,msgtyp,msgflg)


/* semget()-get a set of semaphores */

#include sys\types.h

#inlcude sys\ipc.h

#include sys\sem.h

key_t    key;              /* key for semaphore set */
```

```
int      nsems,              /* number of semaphores in set */
         semflg;             /* semaphore status */
int      semget(key,nsems,semflg);


/* semctl()-semaphore control ooperations */
#include sys\types.h

#include sys\ipc.h

#include sys\sem.h

int      semid,              /* semaphore identifier */
         cmd;                /* control operation */
int      semnum;            /* number of semaphore in set */
union    semun
                {
                int     val;     /* value to set semaphore to */
                struct  semid_ds *buf;  /* semaphore data structure */
                ushort  *array; /* set semaphore values according to
                                array */
                } arg;
int      semctl(semid,semnum,cmd,arg)


/* shmget()-get shared memory segment */
#include sys\types.h

#inlcude sys\ipc.h

#include sys\shm.h

key_t    key;               /* key for shared memory segment */
int      shmflg:            /* message status *.
```

```
int        size;                /* size of memory segment */

int        shmget(key,size,shmflg)


/* shmctl()-shared memory control operations */

#include sys\types.h

#include sys\ipc.h

#include sys\shm.h

int        shmid,               /* shared memory identifier */

           cmd;                 /* control operation */

struct     shmid_ds *buf;       /* shared memory data structure */

int        shmctl(shmid,cmd,buf)


/* shmop-shared memory operations */

/* shmat()-attach shared memory segment */

#include sys\types.h

#include sys\ipc.h

#include sys\shm.h

int        shmid;               /* shared memory identifier */

char       *shmaddr;            /* address to attach segment to */

int        shmflg;              /* status of memory segment */

int        shmat(shmid,shmaddr,shmflg)


/* shmdt()-detach form calling process data segment */


#include sys\types.h

#include sys\ipc.h
```

```
#include sys\shm.h

char      *shmaddr;         /* address of segment to detach */

int       shmdt(shmaddr)
```

Summary

Because processes in the UNIX environment are distinct and individual units with private data, facilities must be provided to allow the processes to communicate between themselves. The reason for interprocess communication can be either to simply exchange data, or to synchronize the execution of specific events. UNIX provides seven mechanisms for interprocess communications.

Signals indicate to processes the occurrence of some specific event. Signals are not queued and are processed only while a process is running, so multiple signals sent to a non-executing process will be lost. Process tracing is typically a debugging tool. It provides a mechanism for a parent process to specifically control the execution of a child process—providing breakpoint mechanisms and similar devices for fine control. Pipes are provided in two varieties. Unnamed pipes are created when a pipeline is specified on the command line. Named pipes are created by specific system calls. All pipes are FIFO files with data from one process being poured into one end of the pipeline and the receiving process drawing the data out of the other end. Semaphores are a sophisticated form of signals with a variety of event postings possible. Messages provide the ability for processes to share large volumes of free format data. Shared memory provides the capability for multiple executing processes to use a portion of the same data area.

All interprocess communication is controlled via system calls to the kernel. The kernel handles the interprocess communication on behalf of the requesting process.

Points to Ponder

Consider the use of process tracing in a context outside of debugging. What would be an appropriate use of this interprocess communication facility?

Shared memory is extremely fast and efficient—it also has the potential for being destructive and dangerous. Design an algorithm that couples one or more of the other interprocess communication facilities with shared memory to help remove some of its dangers.

Parallel processing (the use of multiple, closely coupled CPU's sharing a copy of the same operating system) is becoming a very important technology. How would the UNIX interprocess communication facilities be of value to controlling multiple CPU's in such an environment?

5

The Lives of A Process

Processes are programs running in the UNIX environment. Every executing program is a process and nothing that executes can be anything but a process. The control over process birth, death, and execution is the primary task of the UNIX kernel. Almost all of its other functions support this task.

Processes can only be created by other processes. There is no way for a process to come into being unless it is spawned by an already running process. Having stated this iron-clad rule, it must be said that there are three exceptions to this rule, and they will be discussed here. To begin, however, we will take a closer look at the circumstances involved in the actual creation of a process.

Note that creating a new process is not the same as causing the execution of a new executable file (a.out). Two steps are needed for the execution of a new program or executable file. First a new process must be created and then the appropriate context must be mapped into that runnable process.

A new process is created with the fork( ) system call. At any time, the only processes in the entire UNIX environment which are not created with the fork( ) call are processes 0, 1, and 2. These three processes are created when the system is initialized (or booted). Process 0 is the parent of processes 1 and 2. By definition and by convention, process 1 is the parent of all login processes, and as such is the ancestor of all other processes.

When a new process is created, an almost exact copy of the process that is spawning the new process is made. The spawning process is referred to as the parent process, and the spawned process is the child process. Upon creation, the child process looks virtually identical to the parent. Some of the accounting parameters in the user area of the child process are initialized, but most importantly the text, data and stack segments of the child are precisely the same as those of the parent.

THE fork( ) SYSTEM CALL

The fork( ) system call causes several events to occur as it creates a new process. First, it checks to see if enough memory is available on the swap device for the new process. The fork( ) call then calls the *newproc( )* function to allocate a new process table entry. Once the process table entry has been created, newproc( ) creates a copy of the swapping image of the parent. It also initializes certain accounting parameters in the user area of the child process.

In the new process table entry, the new process I.D. of the child process is recorded in p__pid. The process I.D. of the parent or spawning process is recorded in p__ppid. The process I.D. for a new process will always be a unique number between 0 and the maximum process I.D. (usually 30,000, referred to as *MAXPID*). It is worth noting that internally, process I.D.s are used only for interprocess communications. The rest of the time, the process table is searched to locate a particular process by address, or the process is currently running and is recorded in u__procp.

It can be seen from this description that the newproc( ) function is like an internal version of fork( ). It performs the jobs involved in actually creating a new process. It first gets a unique process I.D. and finds an empty entry in the process table. It fills the process table entry for the child process by copying the information from the parent process and by initializing some fields. The newproc( ) function then allocates memory on the swap device for the child's swapping image. The parent's swapping image is copied to the space allocated on the swap device for the child's image. Finally, the new copy of the parent, the child, is added to the run queue and made executable.

If everything were to stop here, the child would be an exact running copy of the parent. This is not a bad thing. There are times when it is necessary to make copies of the parent process. It is also interesting to note that the last task of newproc( ) is to make the child executable. If the creation process is interrupted for any reason, the child will not be. Until the complete copy is finished the process is not executable.

Not every process table entry is left exactly as it was in the parent process. Certain fields are initialized. Figure 5-1 shows the values of the significant new process table entries after initialization is complete. It can be seen from the figure that the child process automatically inherits the same user I.D. as its parent. Note also that while the child inherits the same nice value, it does not use p__cpu (the time running) to compute its priority.

EXECUTING A NEW PROGRAM

The first step in executing a new program is to execute the fork( ) system call. That step creates a new and executable process. Once the process is

Process Table Entry	Value In Parent	Value In Child
Process Status	p_stat	SRUN
Time Running	p_cpu	p_cpu
Memory status flag	p_flag	SLOAD
User I.D.	p_uid	p_uid
Group	p_grp	p_grp
Nice value	p_nice	p_nice
Process I.D.	p_pid	new unique id
Parent process I.D.	p_ppid	p_pid
Time in memory	p_time	0
Priority	p_pri	PUSER + p_nice - NZERO

Fig. 5-1. Values of significant process table entries.

created, its context must be changed to cause a new executable file to run when that process runs. The exec( ) system call performs this task.

The exec( ) system call replaces the text and data portion of the swapping image of the new process with the text and data segments of the executable file to be run. It then allocates a new stack and replaces it on the old stack segment. The exact steps followed by the exec( ) system call are described below.

First the name of the new executable file must be translated so that the appropriate inode for this file can be located. This task is performed by a system call called *namei( )* which will be described in detail in a later chapter. Next the permissions for the executable file are checked to be sure that the user requesting the execution is allowed to do so. The size of the program is checked to make sure that it can be loaded at this time.

Next, any arguments to the new program are collected and stored on the swap device. Memory is set up for the new executable program, overlaying the memory for the new process. The text segment for the executable program is read and loaded into the appropriate area of the new process. This is not a trivial task. In particular, the shared text model must be tested for, and if the shared text is found to be operational, the text is loaded only as needed.

Following the loading of the text segment, the data segment for the new executable file is loaded. The argument list is copied from the swap device to the stack and the swap space used for the arguments is deallocated. Finally, all the signals are set to default status and the registers are reset.

At this point in the execution of a new program, a new executable file has been loaded and is ready to run. The process created by the fork( ) call was in proper status. The new context with text and data for the new executable program has effectively overlayed the process just created. Now the new executable file will run.

PROCESS TERMINATION

As would be expected, termination of a process is a relatively easier job than creation of a process. The major activity in terminating a process is the deallocation of the swapping image of that process. The only complication in the deallocation of the swapping image of a process occurs when the text or a portion of the memory is shared. In that case, the portion of the swapping image that is shared is not deallocated.

It is possible that for a variety of reasons the process table entry for a process could remain in memory after the swapping image has been deallocated. This would occur if the parent needed information about the child process after the death of the child.

There are two ways to cause the death of a process. One of these ways is to send a signal to the process with the action set to default on receipt. Since the default action is death, this is a simple way to cause the termination of a process. The other way to terminate a process is with the *exit( )* system call. Both of these trigger the death sequence.

Once the death of a process has been called for, the process turns itself into what is called a *zombie process*. In this state, we appropriately describe the process as dead but not buried. This means that the process has no swapping image, but it still exists in the process table, which gives it a dubious and not very useful status. The zombie can be laid to rest, that is, have its process table entry removed, by its parent or stepparent using the wait( ) system call. The zombie can never be made executable again since it has no swapping image.

When a child dies, the parent is informed of that death via a *SIGCLD* signal. When that signal is received, the parent should remove the child entry from the process table. In the event that the parent dies before the child, the child is inherited by process 1. Process 1, a child of process 0, is the ancestor of all processes except process 0 and is the stepparent of all orphaned processes. If for any reason the parent of a process does not remove the process table entry for a dead child, then it is up to process 1 to remove that table entry.

The tasks performed by the exit( ) system call are shown in Fig. 5-2.

PROCESS STATES

A process can only be found in a finite number of states during the course of its lifetime. Figure 5-3 shows the various lives of a process in the case of the most natural course of events, and Fig. 5-4 shows the possible transitions between the states described in Fig. 5-3.

OF INTEREST TO PROGRAMMERS

The fork( ) system call is used to create a new process which is identical to its parent. The syntax for the fork( ) system call is

    int fork( )

The return from fork( ) to the parent is the process I.D. of the new child process.

1) Set the action for all signals to ignore for the process to be terminated.

2) Close all files opened by the process to be terminated.

3) Deallocate the swapping image of the terminating process.

4) Set the status of the terminated process to zombie: p_stat == SZOMB.

5) Notify the parent of the death of a child by the SIGCLD signal.

6) Cause the child to be disowned by the parent by setting the I.D. of the parent process to 1 (ppid == 1).

7) Notify process 1 if a zombie child exists.

8) Cause a switch to a new process to occur.

Fig. 5-2. Tasks performed by the exit ( ) system call.

1) The process is newly created. It exists but is neither sleeping nor ready to run. This is the state of a process during, but prior to completion of the fork() system call.

2) The process is executable on the swap device.

3) The process is in main memory, is executable, but is not currently running.

4) The process is executing in user mode.

5) The process is running in kernel mode.

6) The process is moving from kernel mode to user mode, but has been preempted.

7) The process is sleeping in main memory.

8) The process is sleeping on the swap device.

9) The process is a zombie, no longer executable.

Fig. 5-3. The lives of a process.

Current Process State

Transition to		1	2	3	4	5	6	7	8	9
		A	B	C	D	E	F	G	H	I
1	A									
2	B	x	x	x					x	x
3	C		x	x	x	x	x	x		x
4	D		x	x	x		x	x		
5	E		x	x	x	x				
6	F									
7	G		x	x	x		x		x	
8	H		x					x		
9	I									x

Fig. 5-4. Illustration of the Current Process state.

When it is time to execute a new program, first the fork( ) must be issued and then the exec( ) system call must be used to copy the text and data of the new executable file. There are several forms of the exec( ) system call. Different forms should be selected depending on the nature and number of arguments involved and the system environment at the time of the call. It is important to note that the actual action of the exec( ) system call is to transform the calling process into the new executable file. Thus an exec( ) with no fork( ) will transform the only copy of the calling process into the new executable file. The available forms of exec( ) are shown in Fig. 5-5.

When it is time to terminate a process the exit( ) system call should be used. Both the exit( ) and wait( ) calls should be used as described in the previous chapter.

```
char        *path,    /* pointer to path name identifying new process f
            *arg0,    /* null terminated character string argument */
            *arg1,
                .
                .
                .
            *argn;
int         execl(path,arg0,arg1,...,argn, (char *)0)

char        *path,
            *argv[];             /* array of argument strings */
int         execv(path,argv)

char        *path,    /* pointer to path name identifying new process f
            *arg0,    /* null terminated character string argument */
            *arg1,
                .
                .
                .
            *argn,
            *envp[];             /* environment of new process */
int         execl(path,arg0,arg1,...,argn, (char *)0,envp)

char        *path,
            *argv[],
            *envp[];
int         execve(path,argv,envp)

char        *file,    /* pointer to path name identifying new process f
            *arg0,    /* null terminated character string argument */
            *arg1,
                .
                .
                .
            *argn;
int         execlp(file,arg0,arg1,...,argn, (char *)0)

char        *file,
            *argv[];             /* array of argument strings */
int         execvp(file,argv)
```

Fig. 5-5. Forms of the exec( ) system call.

The most important aspect of this chapter for programmers is that only
processes create processes. The processes thus inherit much of their
information from their parent. This close parent/child kinship must always be
considered when developing applications in the UNIX environment. The
organization of groups and owners must be carefully considered to allow the
proper control among the various processes in an application.

Summary

Controlling the birth, life and death of processes is the primary function of the UNIX kernel. The rule most beneficial in exerting this control is that all new processes must be spawned by already existing processes. Process 1 in the process table is one of only three processes which do not follow this rule. It is created when the system is initialized and is the parent of all login processes and thus is the ancestor of all processes.

The fork( ) system call creates an exact duplicate of itself. This duplicate or child shares all the same parameters as its parent. To cause the execution of a new process, the exec( ) system call is invoked following the fork( ) call. The exec( ) call replaces the text and data portions of the new process with the text and data of the process image to be executed.

Processes die either by killing themselves (via an exit( ) call) or by being killed with the kill( ) signal. The first event in the death of a process is the removal of its swapping image from memory. If information about a process remains in the process table following its death, the process is referred to as a zombie.

Points to Ponder

The BSD UNIX version provides a vfork( ) call which assumes that exec( ) will always immediately follow the fork( ). Thus vfork( ) effectively does a fork( ) and exec( ). What is the benefit of such a command? What are its potential liabilities?

Under what circumstances might a parent die before a child? What happens to the child in that case?

UNIX Files and Inodes

The UNIX kernel ultimately views all files as streams of bytes. Internally, however, UNIX does distinguish between four types of files. This discrimination between files relates to the way the system handles the file storage structures and controls the data flowing to and from the files.

The *regular* file type is the most familiar. It is the source or object code for a program or the text of a document. Regular files are also referred to as ASCII files. *Directory*-type files contain the list of filenames in any particular directory along with the associated inode numbers for those files. Directory files are the roadmaps for locating files in the file system. *Special* files are those files which are actually other devices—such as disk drives, terminals and printers. Finally, the fourth type of file is the *named pipe*, which in most ways is a subset of the regular file type except for its FIFO organization.

Regular files are totally user-definable and controllable. The operating system makes no assumptions and imposes no constraints on the structure of regular files. These files contain data inserted into them by the user or by user programs. The structure and content of these files is entirely user-defined. Most importantly, these files are entirely read and written by the user—assuming that appropriate read and write privileges apply.

Directory files contain the data needed to map file names to the contents of the files. The structure of directory files is controlled by the operating system; it cannot be modified by any user or user program. Directory files are readable by users, but only the operating system can write to the directory file.

One of the real benefits of the UNIX operating system is that it views everything as a file. Thus, the special devices—the terminals, disks, printers etcetera—are represented by special files. Special files are actually the data stored in and sent from the device the file represents. These files map the file names to the devices supported by the UNIX system. Four types of devices are represented by special files: character, block, raw block (non-buffered), and terminal I/O. With the appropriate permissions, special files can be read from and written to by users and user programs.

Named pipes, the fourth file type, contain any type of data placed in them by user or operating system programs. The major restriction on named pipes is that they never contain more than 10 blocks of data. Inasmuch as these files contain data placed in them by user programs, the structure of these files is user-controlled. Named pipes are user-read and -write, again given that the appropriate permissions exist.

The common element these four files share is that they are all administered through inodes. An inode should be viewed as an information node for each file. These inodes contain the administrative data necessary for each file and its use by the system.

INODES

Administrative information for each file is contained in the inode for that file. Files and file names should not be confused. Several file names may be associated with one inode, but an active inode is associated with exactly one file. This makes it possible, for example for a physical disk file to be accessed by several different names, each of these names associated with a common inode.

The attributes of the file as well as its permissions and other administrative data are stored in the inode. In addition, the inode contains the addresses of the physical file data. Inodes are always resident on the disk, and as they are used they may also be resident in memory.

Specifically, a disk-resident inode contains the information in Fig. 6-1. The variables in the kernel code referring to disk resident inode information always begin with the di__ characters. All of the information in the disk-resident inode structures is stored as integers.

The file mode is a two-byte bit flag. The first nine bits of this flag store the access and execution permissions associated with the file. Bits 0 through 8 are broken into three 3-bit clusters. Bits 0 through 2 are the permissions for the "others," bits 3 through 5 are the permissions for the "group" and bits 6 through 8 are the owner permissions. The meaning of bits 0 through 8 is shown in Fig. 6-2.

Bits 9 through 11 are the execution flags. For example, the set user I.D. on the execution flag is set in this bit cluster. Bits 12 through 14 indicate the file type. These last three bits describe whether the file is a regular type, a directory, character or block special file, or a FIFO (pipe) file.

The *link count field* indicates how many directory references there are to

```
file mode           di_mode
link count          di_nlink
owner id            di_uid
group id            di_gid
file size           di_size
file addresses      di_addr[0]
                         .
                         .
                         .
                    di_addr[39]
last accessed       di_atime
last modified       di_mtime
inode modified      di_ctime
```

Fig. 6-1. Information in a disk-resident inode.

the inode and therefore to the physical file. A link count of zero indicates an unallocated inode. Every file must have a link count of at least one. A directory file must have a link count of at least two (one from the parent and one from itself—the . and .. entries in the directory). Whenever a file is accessed by a new name (using the link command) the link count is incremented. Whenever a file name is deleted (or unlinked) the link count is decremented. When the link count drops to zero, the file becomes inaccessible and is gone forever.

The two I.D. fields contain information indicating the ownership and group I.D.s associated with the file. Of course, the superuser has full access to all files.

The *file size field* contains the number of bytes in the file. This will always be zero for a special file. It will accurately reflect the size of regular, directory and pipe files.

The *time stamps field* contains the number of seconds since 00:00:00 Greenwich Mean Time on January 1, 1970. The reason for maintaining this

Bit	Meaning
8	Owner Read Permission
7	Owner Write Permission
6	Owner Execute Permission
5	Group Read Permission
4	Group Write Permission
3	Group Execute Permission
2	Other Read Permission
1	Other Write Permission
0	Other Execute Permission

Fig. 6-2. Bits storing access and execution permissions.

number of seconds is to show the time a file was last accessed in any way. The last time a file was modified, and the last time the inode was modified are also indicated through this means. It is possible to modify an inode without accessing or modifying a file. Incidentally, linking a new name to a file causes the link count to be incremented without affecting the file at all.

FILE ADDRESSES

The inode for a file contains the physical disk address of that file. Files under UNIX do not require contiguous storage areas, nor the pre-allocation of space. Thus files may be stored in many separate areas of the disk. The inode contains 39 bytes of address information. These 39 bytes are used to point either directly or indirectly to the addresses in which the file is stored.

The one fixed element of UNIX file storage is that files are broken into as many one block pieces as is needed to store them. These blocks are then placed at whatever free blocks are available. The size of a block on most UNIX systems is usually 512 or 1024 bytes, and is stored in the system constant BLOCKSIZE. Thus on a system using a 1024-byte block, a file containing 8000 bytes would require eight blocks of physical storage. These eight blocks would not necessarily be contiguous, but would be individually addressed from the inode.

For regular and directory type files, the 39 bytes of address information space in the inode is broken into 13 three-byte fields. The first ten of these fields (fields 0-9, bytes 0-29) contain addresses of the physical disk blocks containing file data. The 8000-byte file mentioned above would, in this instance, be entirely addressed by the first eight addresses stored in these fields. These first ten fields are referred to as direct block addresses.

The eleventh field (field 10, bytes 30-32) contains the address of a block containing the direct block address. This is referred to as an indirect block address. The block pointed to by this field can contain up to BLOCKSIZE/3 direct block addresses.

The twelfth field (field 11, bytes 33-35) is a double *indirect block address*. As would be expected, a double indirect block address points to a block containing the addresses of indirect block addresses (as does field 10). It is referred to as double because it is literally doubly indirect—the twelfth field contains an address that points to an address—a double address direction. The block pointed to by this field can contain up to BLOCKSIZE/3 indirect block addresses.

Finally, the thirteenth field (field 12, bytes 36-38) is a triple indirect block address. It points to a block containing double indirect block addresses which in turn point to blocks of indirect block addresses which then point to blocks of direct block addresses—making it triply, or thrice-removed from the actual address. These concepts are illustrated in Fig. 6-3.

At first this may seem a rather obscure and limited approach to storing and accessing data files. Consider, however, the case of a system with a blocksize of 1024 bytes. In this example, let us further assume that each block can be accessed by a four-byte integer. Block addresses are stored in three bytes in the disk resident inode, but are converted to four bytes in memory. Thus, the ten direct address blocks store addresses for a file up to the size of 10k bytes.

The next field, the indirect address block, can hold up to 256 block addresses (1024/4 = 256), so the maximum file size is now 256k (from the indirect address block) plus the 10k directly addressed for a total of 266k bytes. The double indirect adds another 256 indirect blocks or 256 times 256 direct

```
:        Direct Block Addresses                 :
:_____: _____
:000:001:002:003:004:005:006:007:008:009:010:011:012:
----------------------------------------------------
    :   :   :   :   :   :   :   :   :   :   :   :   :
    : <--: <--: <--: <--: <--: <--: <--: <--: <--:   :   :   :
    :                                           :   :   :
    :   Indirect                                :   :   :
    :   Block                                   :   :   :
    :   Addresses                               :   :   :
    :                                           :   :   :
    :   ---------                               :   :   :
    : :       :                                 :   :   :
    : : : : : : : <----------------------------:   :   :
    :   : ---------:  Double                        :   :
    : <-------:    ^   Indirect                     :   :
    :             :   Block                         :   :
    :             :   Addresses                     :   :
    :             :                                 :   :
    :             :   ---------                     :   :
    :             : :       :                       :   :
    :             :---: : : : : : <----------------:   :
    :                 :---------:                      :
    :                         ^   Triple              :
    :                         :   Indirect            :
    :                         :   Block               :
    :                         :   Addresses           :
    :                         :                       :
    :                         :   ---------           :
    :                         : :       :             :
    :                         :---: : : : : : <---------:
    :                             :----------:
    :
    \ /
File Data Blocks
------------------------------------------
: : : : : : : : : : : : : : : : : : :
------------------------------------------
```

Fig. 6-3. Block addresses.

blocks for an additional 64M bytes. Finally the triple indirect block adds yet another 256 double indirect blocks, providing a maximum file size of well over 16 gigabytes.

This storage-access approach obviously lends itself to very large files when required. However, accessing a specific data block which is pointed to through triple indirection can be a cumbersome and time-consuming process since as many as four distinct disk accesses may be required to ultimately retrieve the desired data. Again, for typical UNIX systems, this does not appear to be a problem. A study done by Mullender and Tannenbaum (Mullender, S.J. A.S. Tanenbaum, "Immediate Files," *Software-Practice and Experience*, Volume 14(4), April 1984) indicates that 48 percent of all files on a UNIX system are less than 1k bytes and a full 85 percent of files on a UNIX system are less than 8k bytes. Therefore, it can be said in general that most files on typical UNIX systems are addressable directly from the inode block pointers.

The addresses in the inode are used somewhat differently for special files and named pipes. The inode address space is organized into the same 13 fields for named pipes. However named pipes are limited to 10k bytes so that only the direct address fields are needed to address the file itself. Initially the last three fields are set to zero. These fields are ultimately used, however, and their usage will be detailed in Chapter 9.

Only the first two of the 39 address bytes are used for special files. The field di__addr[0] contains the channel number of the device or the minor device number. The major device type, which is the integer value of the device type, is stored in the field di__addr[1]. The other address fields are unused.

OF INTEREST TO PROGRAMMERS

Programmers need to be aware of three major factors described in this chapter: the relationship of the inode to the file, the file-data addressing scheme and its impact on data retrieval, and finally the size limitations on named pipes and the implications of those limitations.

The programmer must consider that the name of a file is simply a pointer to the inode for that file. Since multiple file names can point to a single inode, it is possible for a file to be referenced by several names. Every file must have at least one name (a link count of one). When the link count goes to zero, the inode is no longer associated with the physical file and the data in that file is no longer retrievable.

Files of up to 10k bytes are directly addressable from the inode. Thus access speeds will be best when the data to be retrieved resides in that 10k of direct addressability. Extremely large files can be handled by the UNIX operating system, however, as a general rule several smaller files are better than a large file if access speed is a major concern.

Finally, named pipes are limited to 10k bytes. This limitation ensures fast access to the information in the named pipe, but it may also cause the pipe to fill quickly if large amounts of data are being passed. When data volumes exceeding 10k bytes at one time are being passed between processes the programmer should consider whether a named pipe is appropriate—or perhaps on a more basic level, if the design which led to such a large volume of interprocess data transfer is sound.

Summary

While the kernel views everything as a file, and therefore as a stream of bytes, there are four distinguishable file types on the UNIX system. The distinguishing factors are file content and structure. The predominant types of file is the regular file, which is user defined. The directory type file contains file names and i-numbers for those file names. Named pipes contain any type of data but are FIFO in nature. The special files are actually conduits for data flowing to and from devices such as printers, terminals, disk and tape drives, and even memory.

The data structure common to all UNIX files is the inode. The inode contains the administrative data relating to a file and it contains the disk addresses for the file. Files in UNIX are stored in one block chunks, with each block pointed directly to or indirectly from the inode. The inode contains a series of bytes which contain the physical disk addresses of the first eight blocks of data. It also contains the address of one indirect block, one double indirect block and one triple indirect block. The indirect blocks point in turn to blocks containing disk addresses.

Points to Ponder

Storing data in small, one block segments while efficiently using disk space, limits the size of a single file and can result in increased overhead during file retrieval. The BSD UNIX version uses large blocks and allows fragments of several files to be stored in a single block. What are the advantages and disadvantages of this approach?

Why is it important that everything look like a file to the UNIX kernel?

7

The UNIX File System

UNIX files are accessed and controlled by inodes. The overall organization of these files and inodes is called the UNIX file system. The file system was one of the major focuses of the UNIX developers. It is a pivotal point in UNIX architecture. Along with process control, the file system is one of the most significant aspects of the UNIX operating system.

The file system provides a structure for the collection of all the files in a system. Since the kernel views virtually everything as a file at some level, the file system can be said to comprise the overall system organization.

The file system provides a mechanism for uniquely identifying each file and for logically separating the files for purposes of security and backup. Because of the file system, it is possible to work with individual files instead of all the data on a particular device. The UNIX file system, in addition to providing for file identification and logical separation, also provides physical separation of file systems.

While it is convenient to refer to the UNIX file system, this is not entirely accurate. UNIX supports multiple file systems. One file system is in control or in charge of the UNIX-system startup and initialization, but other file systems may also be added on or removed. It is possible to define a single physical device (such as a disk drive) into several file systems. It is also possible to define a separate device as a file system and then join it with the primary file system (through a process known as *mounting*). In general it can presently be said that a file system cannot span multiple physical devices. In other words, if a physical disk device can store ten megabytes of data, then that is the physical limit of the size of the file system on that device. This may change in the near future.

A FILE SYSTEM: THE EXTERNAL VIEW

A file system gives the appearance of being a hierarchical structure. File systems are often referred to in terms of trees or inverted trees and these are convenient metaphors.

Every file system has a *root directory*. This root directory, like a parent process, is the point of growth for all other directories in a file system. The file system directory is merely a file which associates file names with inodes. Every directory except the root has a parent directory. Every directory can have one or more children. A child is another directory, referenced in the parent. In addition to child directories, a directory can reference regular files, special files, or named pipes. A pictorial representation of a file system appears in Fig. 7-1.

Every file in a file system can be accessed either by specifying either its *full path* or a *relative path*. The path is the list of directories which must be traversed in order to locate the specified file. For many UNIX users, this external view is as complete a picture of the file system as is ever necessary.

A FILE SYSTEM: THE INTERNAL VIEW

A file system is a collection of contiguous disk blocks. Included in these blocks are a *boot block*, a *super block*, a collection of *inode blocks*, *inode control blocks*, and *data blocks*. The location of some of these blocks is critical.

The first block in a file system is the boot block. The second block is the superblock. Following the super blocks come the inode and inode control blocks (called the *i_list*) followed by the data blocks. This relationship between blocks will always be true in a UNIX file system. Figure 7-2 lists the different blocks and describes them.

The boot block is the first block in a UNIX file system. If the file system is the one from which UNIX is being booted, then the boot block will be used.

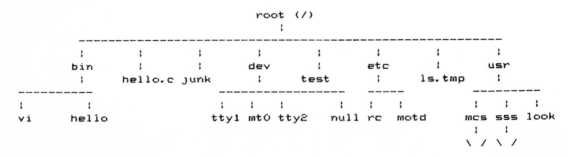

Fig. 7-1. Representation of a file system.

```
Block                    Description

   0                     Boot Block
   1                     Superblock
   2
   .
   .                     i_list Blocks
   .
 FD-1                    Last i_list Block
  FD                     First Data Block
   .
   .                     Data Blocks
   .
 T-1
   T                     Total Blocks in File System
```

Fig. 7-2. UNIX File System Blocks.

It will contain the boot program and other information necessary for the initialization of the UNIX system. If the file system is not the one from which UNIX is being booted, then block 0 is unused and unusable. In this case the actual contents of block 0 are undefined.

The superblock contains a complete catalog of specific information about the file system (and will be described in detail later). The superblock is always the second block in the file system. In general terms, the superblock contains data reflecting the state of the file system—its size, how many files may be stored, where to find free space, and so on.

The i__list blocks are the list of inodes for the file system. The number of inodes is specified by the system administrator when the system is configured. An inode is 64 bytes long so the number of i__list blocks depends on the number of inodes specified. Unlike regular file storage, the i__list is contiguous and always follows the superblock.

The data blocks, which make up the largest portion of the file system, begin immediately following the i__list and consume the rest of the blocks in the file system. Generally speaking, the ratio of data blocks to i__list blocks is approximately 4:1. There is no structure or organization to the data blocks. Each data block in use will be pointed to by an inode. The data blocks hold primarily user-created or -defined data, although system data is stored in the data blocks as required.

THE DISK-RESIDENT SUPERBLOCK

As with inodes, the superblock has both a disk-resident and a memory-resident form. The disk-resident superblock contains administrative information for use during a file system mount and during the use of certain UNIX system utility commands (in particular, the *file system check*, or *fsck* command). It is the superblock which tracks free and used data and inode space, and device-specific information as it relates to the file system. It is the primary source of data about all aspects of the file system. Figure 7-3 lists the disk-resident fields found in the superblock.

Clearly, not all of the fields are used when the superblock is disk-resident, nor are all fields meaningful until the file system is actively being used. The

```
Field              Description

s_isize            First data block
s_fsize            Total number of blocks in the file system
s_nfree            Number of free blocks in free block list
s_free[0]          Head of free block chain
s-free[1]
  .
  .                Free block address list
  .
s_free[49]
s_ninode           Number of free inodes
s_inode[0]
s_inode[1]
  .
  .                Free inode number list
  .
s_inode[99]
s_flock            Free block list lock flag (uses only in
                   memory resident version)
s_ilock            Free inode list lock flag (used only in
                   memory resident version)
s_fmod             Superblock modified flag (used only in
                   memory resident version)
s_ronly            Mounted as read only flag (used only in memory
                   resident version)
s_time             Last time super block written to secondary
                   storage device
s_info[0]          Rotational gap
s_info[1]          Blocks/cylinder
s_info[2]          Device specific information
s_info[3]          Device specific information
s_tfree            Number of free data blocks
s_tinode           Number of free inodes
s_fname[0]
  .
```

Fig. 7-3. Disk-resident superblock structure.

86

```
.                    Name of file system when mounted
.
s_fname[5]
s_fpack[0]
.
.                    Name of physical volume
.
s_fpack[5]
s_fill[0]
.
.                    Filler (to make superblock 512 bytes)
.
s_fill[12]
s_magic              FsMAGIC (0xfd187e20--if file system is
                     UNIX V variety)
s_type               1--512 byte block;
                     2--1024 byte block;
                     3--512 byte physical block, 1024 byte logical block
```

superblock has no bearing on system operations, and the file system is not available until the file system is mounted.

FILE SYSTEM MISCELLANY

By definition, inode number 1 is always unused. Inode number 2 is always the root directory of the file system. Thus, as inodes are assigned to other files, they will be assigned beginning with inode number 3. The mechanism by which inodes are assigned will be described later.

File systems can exist on any type of memory device. Traditionally, file systems are located on disk devices. Tape devices could be used to store a file system, but this is not reasonable. The random-access nature of a file system makes a serial-read device such as a tape drive inconvenient and slow at best. The only exception to this is if the file system is primarily archival in nature, or if the application using the file system is dependent upon its serial nature. File systems can be created in physical memory that is, core, and this has been done. Core is generally limited in size, however, thereby limiting file capacity.

File systems are created by the system administrator using the *mkfs* (make file system command). This command takes this form:

/etc/mkfs device #blocks[:#inodes]

The device on which the file system is to be created is named and the total number of blocks in the file system is identified. The system administrator may specify the number of inodes. If the number of inodes (which equates to the maximum number of files) is not specified, the system will compute a default value.

When file systems are created on a disk, they can be created on logical partitions of that disk. A *disk pack* is made up of cylindrical sections logically called cylinders. A group of cylinders can be defined as a *section* and may be assigned a device name (such as /dev/disk10). One file system can be placed on each logical device.

OF INTEREST TO PROGRAMMERS

Construction of the file system should be a point of major concern for programmers. Remember that the locations of the boot block, superblock, i__list and data blocks are fixed relative to each other and to the start of the file system. Even though it is possible to write programs which access specific absolute device addresses directly, direct access to the boot block, superblock or i__list could result in serious system corruption. These areas should be accessed only through the system utilities and through the system calls which will be defined in Chapter 11.

It is also important to remember that inode 1 is never used and inode 2 always refers to the root directory. Again, any effort to circumvent these predefined and fixed definitions will cause unpredictable results.

Summary

The design of the UNIX file system was one of the major concerns of the developers of UNIX. The UNIX file system is the overall structure of file storage and control on the UNIX system. As it exists today, a UNIX system can have multiple file systems, all but one of which would be mountable and dismountable. One file system is the controlling file system from which UNIX is booted.

To the end user, the UNIX file system appears to consist of a root directory and many layers of subdirectories. All subdirectories except the root have exactly one parent directory. A parent can have many children. (Note the parallelism in design between parent and child directories and parent and child processes.)

Internally, the disk organization of the UNIX file system consists of a boot block, a superblock, the i-list and the data blocks. The boot block is only used in the file system from which UNIX is booted. It contains all the bootstrap information necessary to initialize the UNIX system. The superblock contains an up to date status of the file system. The i-list contains a list of all the i-nodes for the file system. The data block contains the actual data.

The system administrator has control of, and responsibility for maintaining and controlling the file systems. It is also the system administrator who can and must verify the state of the file systems with the fsck( ) call.

Points to Ponder

What types of events can cause the superblock to not accurately reflect the state of the file system? What can be done to prevent the superblock from losing synchronization with the file system?

What is the advantage of providing mountable file systems?

There is an optimal relationship between inodes and data blocks. What application and system factors effect the determination of this relationship?

8

The Superblock

The superblock is the second block in all file systems. It contains all the pertinent information about a file system. For a file system to be accessible by the user, the file system must first be mounted. The act of mounting a file system copies the disk-resident superblock into kernel space in primary memory. The reason the superblock is mounted is so that it can provide quick file system information for updates and data access.

The superblock contains a certain amount of miscellaneous information, such as data specific to the device on which the file system is mounted. But it is also and more importantly critical to the maintenance of two specific sets of information. First, it maintains the *free block list*. This is the list of data blocks which are available for use. Secondly, it maintains the *free inode information*, permitting inodes that are available for use to be located quickly when they are needed.

FREE BLOCKS

As soon as a block is needed by a file it is referenced by the inode for that file. *Free blocks* are those blocks not referenced by any inode. The free block list maintained in the superblock is the list of free blocks available to the file system of which that superblock is a member. The list does not maintain free space for an entire device (unless the entire device is the same as the file system).

All free blocks appear in the *free block chain*. The free block chain is initialized when the mkfs command is used to create a file system. The free block chain holds all the free blocks for a file system.

The free block chain is a linked list of *free block address blocks* (similar to indirect inode address blocks). Each free block address block holds up to 50 four-byte addresses of free blocks and a count of the number of free block addresses held. In each free block address block, the zero block is the address of the next free block address block. The superblock entry s_free[0] heads the chain of free block address blocks and points to the next free block address block. Every free block address block has the same structure:

```
struct fblk                                                         {
                                                  int   df_nfree;
                                    d_addr_t df_free[NICFREE];
                                                                    };
```

The entry *df_nfree* contains the count of the number of free address block addresses contained in that block. This number will almost always be 50. The df_free array contains the four-byte addresses of free blocks. NICFREE is a system constant set to 50. The entry df_free[0] points to the next free block address block. If this entry is NULL then the free block chain is terminated. Figure 8-1 illustrates the free block address block chain.

The free block list is maintained in the s_free array of the super block. This list contains a maximum of fifty free block addresses (since s_free[0] is the head of the free block chain, and is therefore used to point elsewhere, there are actually only 49 addresses available for free block addresses). The superblock entry s_nfree contains the number of free blocks in the free block list. Thus, the total number of free blocks on the system (which is contained in s_tfree) can be computed by adding s_nfree and all the df_nfree values.

The s_nfree value serves a double role. Not only does it maintain a count of the number of free blocks, it is also used as an index to retrieve the next free block. Blocks are allocated from the bottom of the free list up. Thus, initially, s_nfree has a value of 50. The next available free block is found at address s_free[s_nfree-1]. As blocks are allocated and the s_nfree value is

```
s_free[0]---df_nfree
              df_free[0]---df_nfree
              df_free[1]    df_free[0]---df_nfree
                    .         df_free[1]    df_free[0]---...---df_nfree
                    .               .         df_free[1]         df_free[0]
                    .               .               .           df_free[1]
              df_free[49]           .               .                 .
                            df_free[49]             .                 .
                                            df_free[49]                .
                                                            df_free[49
```

Fig. 8-1. Diagram of Free Block Address block chain.

92

decremented, the next free block is always s__free[s__nfree-1]. As an added benefit, it is also possible to use the information that the addresses contained in s__free[s__nfree] through s__free[50] are allocated, and moreover, that they are in fact recently allocated.

FREE BLOCK LIST MAINTENANCE

It is not enough for the superblock to have a free list and head a free chain which is correct only when the file system is initialized. The free list must be maintained. Two types of events cause free list maintenance. The free list must be updated whenever a previously free block is allocated, and similarly, maintenance must occur whenever a block previously in use is de-allocated.

The mechanism for maintaining the free list does not allow simultaneous updates to the free list. Measures are taken to prevent two processes from getting the same free block or attempting to free two blocks at the same time and only having one of them recorded. As soon as a process causes free list maintenance, the s__flock flag in the superblock is turned on. This flag ensures that all other processes requesting maintenance will sleep until the list is not being updated.

When blocks are being allocated (and free list allocation always occurs one block at a time), there are two conditions which can occur—the free list can be empty, meaning that there can be insufficient free blocks; or there can be an adequate number of free blocks available.

If there are enough free blocks, then s__nfree will be greater than one. The first step in free block allocation will be to decrement s__tfree. This reduces the count of total system free blocks. The next step is to return the address found at s__free[s__nfree-1]. Finally, s__nfree is decremented. The process requesting the block gets the address returned.

If s__nfree is one, then there are not enough free blocks in the free list. In the case where s__nfree is one the address returned would be s__free[0]. Since this address heads the free block chain, if it were allocated to a process as a free block, all the remaining free blocks on the system would be lost. Therefore, when s__nfree is one and a free block must be allocated, the following steps occur.

First the address at s__free[0] is read. This is the address of the next free block address block. This block is read and the contents on the df__free array are copied into the s__free array. The df__nfree value is copied into the s__nfree value. At this time the new s__free value is probably 50 but it is certainly greater than 1. Free block allocation progresses as usual when there are enough free blocks.

When it is time to de-allocate a block and add it to the free list, there are once again two conditions which can occur. One condition is that there is enough space on the free list to hold another free block address. The other possibility is that the free list is already full.

If the free list is not full, adding a new free block is straightforward. The value s__tfree (total free block count) is incremented. The block address to be added to the list is placed in array entry s__free[snfree]. Finally, snfree is incremented.

When the free list is full, the process of adding a new block is somewhat more complicated. First a new free block address block must be created. Since creating a new free block address block entails getting a free block, the block to be added is considered to be the address of the new free block holding block. The current free list is copied to the new free block address block and the address of the new free block address block is then placed in s__free[0]. The value of s__nfree is set to one and the value of s__tfree is incremented.

HANDLING THE FREE INODE LIST

A free inode is an inode with a zero mode (recall that a zero mode indicates that the inode is unused). Inodes are allocated when a file is created. The process of creating a file causes the inode mode to be changed from zero. The free inode list is maintained in the superblock in the s__inode array. The superblock entry *s__ninode* is the number of free inodes.

A maximum of 100 unallocated inodes are maintained in the superblock i__list. This list is updated and maintained just as the free list is. Similarly to the free list, the i__list cannot be simultaneously updated. The superblock field *s__ilock* is a flag to prevent simultaneous i__list updates. As soon as one process causes an update to the i__list, the s__ilock flag is set, thereby causing any other processes needing an i__list update to sleep until the current update is complete.

It is important to note that there will usually be more than 100 free inodes at any one time. The file system maintains the complete list of inodes in the i__list blocks which follow the superblock and precede the data blocks. Thus, while the addresses of 100 free inodes are stored in the superblock, the disk-resident i__list may contain many more free inodes.

When an inode is to be allocated, there are two cases to be considered. The first case is the simple condition where the superblock free inode list contains a free inode address. This case can be determined easily, since the s__ninode (count of free inodes in the superblock), will be greater than zero. In this case, the address at array location s__inode[s__ninode-1] will be returned. The inode at that location will be initialized and the s__ninode value will be decremented. Finally, the process needing the inode will receive a pointer to that inode.

If s__ninode is zero, then there are no free inodes identified in the superblock. In this case the disk-resident i__list is searched until either 100 free inodes are located, or until all remaining free inodes are located. The s__ninode value is updated to contain the number of free inodes found and the superblock free inode list is filled with the addresses of the just-located free inodes. At this point the superblock free inode list has sufficient free inodes and the allocation process continues as described above.

De-allocating an inode is a relatively simple matter, again with two cases. If the free inode list is not full (that is, s__ninode is less than 100), then the

94

address of the newly freed inode is placed at the array location s__inode[s__ ninode] and the s__ninode value is incremented. If s__ninode is 100, then there is no room for the newly freed inode on the free inode list in the superblock. In this case, the address of the newly freed inode is placed at s__inode[0] if the number of the freed inode is less than that already stored in s__inode[0], otherwise the newly freed inode is not stored in the superblock free inode list. This inode is not lost, since it will be found when it is needed through a search of the disk-resident i__list.

SUPERBLOCK MISCELLANY

There are three informational fields in the superblock which are noteworthy. The flag field s__fmod is set to one every time the superblock is modified. When this field is set on, the next sync( ) system call will write the superblock to disk and reset the s__fmod field. File system inconsistencies and lost data may result if the file system has been modified and the system is then shut down or dismounted without first synchronizing the superblock. This type of condition can occur as the result of abnormal terminations such as power failures. The fsck system utility can be used to resynchronize the file system and the superblock.

The last time the superblock was recorded to secondary storage is reported in the *s__time* field. This field carries the time of the sync( ) system call.

It is possible to mount a file system as read only. In this case the file system could not be modified, but the data would be available for reading. The *s__ronly* flag in the superblock is set to 1 if the file system is mounted as read only.

OF INTEREST TO PROGRAMMERS

The most important aspects of this chapter for programmers are the approaches used for list maintenance for the superblock. The mechanisms used to track, allocate and deallocate free blocks and inodes provide useful algorithms for programmers who will inevitably be faced with similar problems.

It is important to remember that simultaneous updates to the superblock free lists are not possible. Thus, processes doing significant inode or free block maintentance will compete heavily with each other and their individual performance will be degraded. The UNIX system is biased towards applications which require a balanced use of resources. Thus, applications should be designed with resource utilization balance in mind.

Finally, remember that a system shutdown with a modified file system and a non-recorded superblock will result in complex file system maintenance at best and lost data at worst. Every effort should be made to ensure the appropriately timed use of the sync( ) system call. The sync( ) system call is written as it appears below.

```
/* sync—update the super-block */

void sync( );
```

Note that while the use of sync( ) schedules the writing of the superblock to disk, because of competition for system resources the write may not be complete upon return from the call. It is also important to realize that the operating system is somewhat self-protective with regards to the writing of the superblock to disk. The operating system will try to sync( ) the superblock as soon as possible after the setting of the s__fmod flag. In general, applications should not be required to do the sync( ) for themselves, but it can be a good idea in unstable operating environments (or if the *cron* process has been killed).

As a parenthetical note, it has long been a part of UNIX mythology that before shutting down the system the sync shell command should be issued twice, thus:

    $ sync;sync

This has often been questioned. The reason this practice came into being can be explained as follows. The sync shell command invokes the sync( ) system call. A single sync command will take a certain amount of time to actually complete the superblock update. If the system is shut down too quickly, the update will not be complete. Not fully understanding this, operators began to issue a second sync command in an effort to get the timing right on shutting down the system. In reality, a sufficient pause after the first sync command will accomplish the same objective.

Summary

The superblock contains the status of the file system at any time. In particular, it maintains the free block list and the free inode list.

When a file system is mounted, the disk resident superblock is copied into main memory. The sync( ) call is used to write the superblock from main memory back to the disk.

The primary consideration for the kernel regarding the superblock is free list maintenance. When data blocks are needed or freed they must be removed from or added to the free list. Similarly, inodes must be added to and removed from the free inode list as they are used and freed. The one important rule is that simultaneous updates to the free lists are not allowed. If more than one process frees or requires blocks or inodes, they must wait for sequential processing of the free lists.

Points to Ponder

Because the sync( ) call requires physical I/O it is a relatively slow process. This can result in timing problems and superblock corruption. How would you modify superblock processing to help alleviate this problem?

9

Inode and File Tables

The UNIX kernel maintains information essential to the fast and efficient operation of the system in its memory-resident kernel space. Included in the information it maintains is active inode and open file information. This data is stored in tables. The factor common to both tables is that they are not exclusively for a single file system. Both the inode table and the file table store data for all mounted file systems.

THE INODE TABLE

The inode table holds copies of all the active (allocated) i__list inodes. This is a copy of all the i__list inodes which have a non-zero mode. The inodes stored in the inode table are from all the mounted file systems and not from any one file system. Thus, the inode table contains portions of all the i__lists of all mounted file systems.

This inode table provides fast access to the active inodes for efficient reference and modification. It also provides a single inode control point for all processes. The data in the table and the table itself is accessible only via system calls. The following activities use the inode table:

- ☐ I/O (open, read, write, close)
- ☐ File creation
- ☐ Change current directory
- ☐ Mount file system

□ File execution
□ Get file status
□ Change file status
□ Link/unlink file

The inode table is an array of core-resident inode structures. This table resides in kernel space in primary memory. The kernel references the array with the name inode[]. The size of the array is determined by the system administrator during system generation. It is interesting to note that the size of the inode table is not the same as might be indicated by the number of inodes for a file system. This is because the inode table contains only active inodes not for one system, but for multiple file systems. Thus the size of the inode table is the maximum number of files *system-wide* which may require simultaneous access.

In their aspect as core-resident members, the inode structures in the inode table are not identical to the disk-resident structures described in Chapter 6. In general, the disk-resident inode structure is a subset of the core-resident inode structure. The only disk-resident portions of the inode structure which are not maintained in the core-resident structure are the three time fields (last file access time, last file modification time, and last inode modification time). The core-resident structure is illustrated in Fig. 9-1.

The i_forw/i_back and av_forw/av_back are all used to maintain the inode hash chain and/or the free list depending on the hardware on which the UNIX system is being run. The av_forw/av_back fields are used only on the ATT 3B line of computers.

The status of the inode is maintained in the i_flag field. As is common in UNIX this is a bit map field. Figure 9-2 contains a list of the possible status conditions.

Of course, the physical block locations for the file data are still contained in the memory-resident inodes. The full reference to these addresses in the memory-resident inodes is i_blks.ip.i_a[]. This array is the equivalent of the disk-resident i_addr array. The difference between the memory-resident and disk-resident addresses is that the memory-resident addresses are four bytes long instead of three. This conversion is done by the kernel during the reading of the block pointers from the disk.

For regular files and directory files the i_blks.ip.i_a array has 13 elements. The first ten of these elements contain the direct block pointers. The next element contains indirect block pointers. The twelfth element holds double indirect block pointers and the thirteenth element holds triple indirect block pointers. This organization is identical to that of the disk-resident inode.

The inodes for special files do not contain block pointers to data addresses. Only the first array element of the memory-resident inode address array (i_blks.ip.i_a[0]) is used for these files. The element is organized as is shown in Fig. 9-3.

Again, the named-pipes inodes take advantage of the four-byte element size of the memory-resident inode structure. As on the disk, only the first ten

Field	Description
i_forw*	Maintain inode on free list or hash chain
i_back*	Maintain inode on free list or hash chain
av_forw*	Maintain free list
av_back*	Maintain free list
i_flag	bit map
i_count	Total number of references to table entry
i_dev	Major and minor device numbers of device on which inode resides
i_number	Inode number
i_mode	Inode mode (same as di_mode)
i_nlink	Number of directory refernces to inode (same as di_nlink)
i_uid	Owner I.D. (same as di_uid)
i_gid	Group I.D. (same as di_gid)
i_size	File size (same as di_size)
.	
.	
.	
i_blks	Address blocks (same as di_addr[])
.	

Fig. 9-1. The kernel's core-resident structure.

```
   .

   .

i_l                   Address of last successfully read block


   * These fields are hardware dependent.
```

Fig. 9-1. Continued.

```
ILOCK                 Inode locked

IUPD                  File has been updated

IACC                  The last access time needs to be updated

IMOUNT                Inode mounted on

IWANT                 Process sleeping, waiting for inode

ITEXT                 Text prototype inode

ICHG                  Inode modified

ISYN                  Perform synchronous file write
```

Fig. 9-2. Possible inode status conditions.

```
i_blks.ip.i_a[0][0]--Minor device number

i_blks.ip.i_a[0][1]--Major device number

i_blks.ip.i.a[0][2]--Unused

i_blks.ip.i_a[0][3]--Unused
```

Fig. 9-3. First array element of memory-resident inode.

elements of the address are used to contain direct memory addresses. The remaining three array elements are broken into six two-byte fields. The i_blks.ip.i_a structure for named pipe inodes is shown in Fig. 9-4.

The i_frptr field is used to point to the last byte read from the file. The i_fwprt field is used to point to the last byte written to the file. By using these two pointers the kernel can always tell where to read from and write to even though data is constantly being read and written on a FIFO basis.

```
       ----------------------------------------------------------------
00 :             Direct Address Block 0                                 :
       ----------------------------------------------------------------
01 :             Direct Address Block 1                                 :
       ----------------------------------------------------------------
02 :             Direct Address Block 2                                 :
       ----------------------------------------------------------------
03 :             Direct Address Block 3                                 :
       ----------------------------------------------------------------
04 :             Direct Address Block 4                                 :
       ----------------------------------------------------------------
05 :             Direct Address Block 5                                 :
       ----------------------------------------------------------------
06 :             Direct Address Block 6                                 :
       ----------------------------------------------------------------
07 :             Direct Address Block 7                                 :
       ----------------------------------------------------------------
08 :             Direct Address Block 8                                 :
       ----------------------------------------------------------------
09 :             Direct Address Block 9                                 :
       ----------------------------------------------------------------
10 :Unused                          :i_frptr--read pointer              :
       ----------------------------------------------------------------
11 :i_fwptr--write pointer          :i_frcnt--count of reading processes:
   ----------------------------------------------------------------
12 :i_fwcnt--count of writing procs :i_fflag--informational flags       :
       ----------------------------------------------------------------
```

Fig. 9-4. i-blks.ip.i-a structure for named pipe inodes.

In order to avoid redundant or extraneous disk accesses, the system always tries to determine whether it can set up its next read at the same time as it is doing its present read. The i—l field contains the address of the last block successfully read for that particular inode. Use of this field allows the system to determine if the information necessary for the next read is already in memory or if it should be read at the current time.

INODE TABLE MAINTENANCE

The inode table is maintained using two lists. The first of these lists is an *available inode table entry list*. The second is an *allocated inode list*. Both are doubly-linked lists.

The available inode table entry linked list, called *ifreelist*, contains all the unused inode table slots. As soon as the reference count for an inode table slot goes to zero (i—count equal to zero), that slot is linked to the ifreelist. This list is maintained on a last-in first-out basis (*LIFO*). This means that the newly available slot is linked in at the beginning of the list with the i—forw pointer. The available entry list always starts at the address ifreelist that points to the first inode added to the list. When the system is initialized, almost all of the inode table entries are placed on the available entry list.

When an inode is allocated, it is removed from the available list and placed on the allocated inode list. This is also a doubly-linked list. Instead of being headed by a single address as is the available list, this list is headed by an entry in a hash table array called hinode[ ]. This means that there will actually be several allocated inode linked lists, each headed by one of the entries in hinode[ ]. The size of each hash list is usually 128 and is always a power of two.

When a particular inode is needed, the device number (i—dev) is used with the inode number in a hashing algorithm to produce an offset into hinode[ ]. The address contained at this offset is the start of the appropriate allocated inode list. If the inode is found on this list, then a pointer to the inode table entry is returned. If the inode is not found, then a new entry is created in the hash list. A search for a specific inode will always result in either the immediate location of that inode, or in the creation of the inode in the hash list.

In order to make a new hash table entry several steps must occur. The first step is the location of the next available inode. This will be the entry in the available list pointed to by ifreelist. It will also be the last inode de-allocated. This inode must then be removed from the available list and modified to reflect the file type and status for which it is being allocated. Now fully defined, this inode is linked to the end of the appropriate hash list.

Inodes are de-allocated when their reference count drops to zero (i—count equal to zero). When the reference count goes to zero, the inode slot is removed from the hash list of allocated inodes and placed on the available inode list.

THE FILE TABLE

The file table stores specific information for each open file. Table entries are allocated on a "per open" basis. There are three system calls which cause file table entries to be made: open( ), create( ) and pipe( ).

The file table, just like the inode table, is an array of file structures called name[ ]. These structures occupy kernel space in main memory. The number of entries is usually on the order of 100 to 300 and is defined by the system administrator at the time of system generation. It corresponds to the maximum number of files which can be simultaneously open systemwide. This table, like the inode table, reflects the entire system (all mounted file systems) and not just an individual file system.

Four fields make up each entry in the file table. These fields are:

f__flag	Status flag
f__count	Reference count
f__up	Pointer value
f__un	File offset

The f__flag field maintains the file status. It indicates the open status of the file, that is, whether the file was opened for reading, writing, both, etcetera. It is set by several system calls: open( ), create( ), pipe( ), close( ), fcntl( ).

The reference count field (f__count) maintains a count of the total number of file descriptors allocated by processes accessing the file via the file table entry. For example, the dup( ) system call would cause the field to be incremented as it returns a second descriptor for an already opened file. The system calls which can cause this field to be altered are: creat( ), open( ), dup( ), fcntl( ), close( ) and pipe( ).

The pointer value field (f__up) can have two different meanings. If the reference count is greater than zero, meaning the entry is allocated, then f__up points to the corresponding inode. If the reference count is zero, meaning an unallocated or free file table entry, then the pointer points to the next available file table entry. This serves to provide a linked list of unallocated file table entries.

Finally, f__un, the file offset field provides the present position of the read/write pointer within a file. This pointer is shared by all processes accessing a file. It is modified by three system calls: read( ), write( ), and lseek( ).

OVERVIEW OF TABLE CONNECTIONS

The user block contains an array called u__ofile[ ]. These arrays exist for all users and will point to each of the allocated file table entries. In turn, each allocated file table entry points to an entry in the inode table with the f__up field. All of the unallocated file table entries are linked together in a free list pointed to by an entry called *ffreelist* (the corresponding entry to ifreelist). Thus, the user block array *uofile[ ]* contains pointers to the file table entries which through the f__un fields point to the inode table entries. The system calls open( ), create( ), fcntl( ), dup( ) and pipe ( ) provide the offsets into u__ofile[ ].

FILE TABLE ENTRY MANAGEMENT

When it is necessary to allocate a file table entry, the system call falloc( ) does the real work. It gets the value of the entry pointed to by ffreelist and returns it as the file table entry to be allocated. It then adjusts the value of ffreelist so that it points to the next free file table entry.

The *closef( )* system call handles the tasks associated with de-allocating a file table entry. When a file table entry is de-allocated, the value in ffreelist is modified to point to the new free file table entry. This new entry has its f_un value reset to point to the entry previously pointed to by ffreelist.

OF INTEREST TO PROGRAMMERS

The tables described in this chapter greatly influence the efficient operation of the UNIX system. For system administrators, proper system sizing is a critical concern. Allocating too much space to these entries expands the amount of space occupied by the kernel in primary memory. This will reduce the amount of space available for user programs and result in more paging and swapping as processes execute. Conversely, too little space will damage performance by forcing processes into extended wait states while waiting for free inodes or files.

Eleven system calls were described which affect inode and file tables. These calls are presented in alphabetical order at the conclusion of this chapter in Fig. 9-5.

```
np



           /* close--close a file descriptor */



           int fildes;     /* file descriptor of file to be closed */

           int close(fildes)




           /* creat--create a new file or rewrite an existing one */



           char *path;     /* name of file to be created */

           int mode;       /* open mode */

           int creat(path, mode)

           /* dup--duplicate an open file descriptor */



           int fildes;     /* file descriptor of file to be duplicated */
```

Fig. 9-5. System calls affecting inode and file tables. Continued to page 106.

```
int dup(fildes)



/* fcntl--file control */

#include fcntl.h


int fildes,      /* file descriptor of file to be modified */
    cmd;         /* command to be issued:


            F_DUPFD--return a new file descriptor;

            F_GETFD--get the close-on-execution flag;

            F_SETFD--set the close-on-execution flag;

            F_GETFL--get the file status flags;

            F_SETFL--set the file status flags;

            F_GETLK-- get th efirst lock;

            F_SETLK--set or clear the file segment lock;

            F_SETLKW--same as F_SETLK with sleep */

int fcntl(fildes, cmd, arg) /*arg is dependent on cmd */


/* lseek--move read/write status pointer */


int fildes;      /*file descriptor of file to have pointer moved */

long offset;     /* number of bytes to move pointer */

int whence;      /* initial pointer location before offset */

int lseek(fildes, offset, whence)

/* open--open for reading or writing */

#include fcntl.h


char *path;      /* name of file to open */

int oflag,       /* open status */
```

```
        mode;        /* open mode */

int open(path, oflag[ ,mode])


/* pipe--create an interprocess channel */

int fildes[2];   /* file descriptors for reading and writing */

int pipe(fildes)


/* read--read from file */


int fildes;      /* file descriptor of file to be read */

char *buf;       /* buffer to contain data read */

unsigned nbyte;  /* number of bytes actually read */

int read(fildes, buf, nbyte)


/* write--write on a file */

int fildes;      /* file descriptor of file to be written on */

char *buf;       /* buffer containing data to be written */

unsigned nbyte;  /* number of bytes to write */

int write(fildes, buf, nbyte)
```

Summary

Two tables are maintained across all mounted file systems—the inode table and the file table. These tables contain information about all the files and all the inodes in use anywhere on the system.

The inode structure is an array of core-resident inode structures. These inode structures are nearly, but not completely identical to their disk resident counterparts. All of the allocated i_list inodes are maintained in the inode table. The maximum size of the inode table is the maximum number of files systemwide which can be simultaneously accessed. Two doubly linked lists— the inode table entry list and the allocated inode list—are used to maintain the inode table.

The file table contains information for each open file on the system. It is an array of core resident file structures. The maximum number of entries in the file table is the maximum number of files systemwide which can be open simultaneously.

Points to Ponder

What are the tradeoffs involved in allowing large numbers of files and inodes to be maintained in the inode and file tables versus allowing relatively small numbers of files and inodes to be maintained?

Would it be possible to derive this information from the superblock, or superblock information from these tables? If not, what changes would be required to allow such a derivation? Would these changes be beneficial to system performance and reliability?

Mounting the File System

By definition, a file system is simply an organized and contiguous collection of blocks. It is composed of the boot block, the superblock, the i_list and the data blocks. File systems reside on separate logical and physical devices. Until a file system is mounted it cannot be accessed. Once a file system is mounted, the user is able to access the files in the file system.

Before a file system is actually mounted, the file system is a separate logical and physical file hierarchy. The user can always access the files of his own file system, but other unmounted file systems are completely unavailable. An additional and separate file system is mounted and its files become available through use of the mount command. This command is written thus:

/etc/mount /dev/dsk10 /newsys

The mount command names the device on which the new file system resides and the name of the directory on which the file system is to be mounted.

When a mount is attempted it is assumed that the mount is feasible. The directory to be mounted on must exist. The logical and/or file device specified must contain a valid file system. When mounting occurs, the hierarchy of the new file system is logically connected to the hierarchy of the existing file system. The point of the mount is an existing directory in the existing file system. The superblock of the new file system is read into the kernel address space when mounting occurs. The superblock fields which contain information referring to mounts, in particular the *mounted on inode* entry is updated and marked as being mounted. The term "mounted on inode" refers to the inode for the directory on which a mount occurs. Finally, an entry is made in the mount table.

Once a mount is complete, the new file system becomes a logical part of the larger system hierarchy. The path to all files in both file systems becomes available from the original root directory. The new file system is still physically separate however. It may be on a separate disk, and there it will remain, even though it can now be logically accessed from the original system.

Mounting is done on to a directory in the original file system. If that directory contains other files they will not be accessible after the mount. However, those apparently missing files are not gone and if the new file system is dismounted they will again be available. Figure 10-1 illustrates graphically the structure of file systems before, during and after mounting.

Note that in this figure file1 and file2, which were previously available in the directory NEWSYS, are not available after the mount. The directory NEWSYS is now the effective root directory for the newly mounted file system.

THE MOUNT TABLE

The mount table is another table in the kernel space in primary memory. Each active entry in the mount table represents one mounted file system. The mount table serves two major purposes. First, it provides *path name resolution*. This means that it provides information to the internal system subroutines. This information is needed to complete a path name when that path crosses file system boundaries. The mount table's second purpose is to provide a pointer to the superblock for each mounted file system. Thus, the mount table is checked whenever the superblock must be located.

As with the other kernel tables, the mount table is an array of structures. Unlike the the other tables and lists, none of the mount table entries are linked. The number of mount table entries is equal to the maximum number of file systems which may be mounted simultaneously. The typical number of mount table entries is between 12 and 18 and is set by the system administrator at the time of system generation. Each mount table structure has five fields. These fields are listed in Fig. 10-2.

There are three possible status flags for a mount table entry: *in use*, *available* and *intermediate*. An in use entry is one which contains information for an active and mounted file system. An available status means that this entry can be used for mounting a file system. The intermediate status indicates that a mount is in progress. It is important to allow for this intermediate status since mounting is a relatively slow process, possibly relying on several different physical devices to become available before it can be completed. It is not at all unlikely that a second mount could be requested before the first is complete. Flagging a mount table entry as a first step ensures that each mount will use a unique table entry.

The major and minor device numbers of the mounted file system are contained in the *mdev field*. When the getfs( ) call tries to find the superblock

```
            File System A
            (File system from which boot occurs)


                root
                   |
  bin------usr----etc------newsys
     |           |       |          |
    vi     mcs---tem    rc    file1--file2




            File System B
            (File system to be mounted)


                root
                   |
  binb------usrb------etcb------newsysb
     |           |           |           |
    vi      mcs---tem       rc      file1--file2




            File System A And B
            (File system after mount)


                root
                   |
  bin------usr----etc------newsys
     |           |       |          |
    vi     mcs---tem    rc       (root)
                                     |
                 binb------usrb------etcb------newsysb
                    |           |           |          |
                   vi      mcs---tem       rc     file1--file2
```

Fig. 10-1. Effect of file system mount.

```
m_flags            Array status
m_dev              Major and minor device numbers of mounted arrays
m_inodp            Address of inode table entry that is mounted on
m_bufp             Address of buffer containing superblock of
                   mounted file system
m_mount            Address of inode table entry that contains root
                   mounted file system
```

Fig. 10-2. Mount table fields.

for a file system, the major and minor device numbers are used to find the correct mount table entry.

The address of the inode on which the new file system is mounted is stored in m_inodp. When a directory is mounted on, the inode for that directory has its IMOUNT status bit set. The address in this entry is the address of the inode with the IMOUNT bit set on for this file system. When a path is being searched to locate a file, as soon as the IMOUNT bit is set the search is directed through the mount table to locate the appropriate root inode.

The address of the superblock buffer for the mounted file system is contained in m_bufp. When the superblock for a file system is needed, this address is used. Note that the buffer containing the superblock does not exist in any other buffer chain.

The inode for the root directory of the mounted file system is found at the address contained in *mmount*. Whenever a path search is directed through the mount table it will continue at the inode to which m_mount is pointing.

OF INTEREST TO PROGRAMMERS

Mounting file systems and tracing paths through the mount system can be a slow process. Because file systems are generally on separate physical devices, when several file systems are involved access times can be quite slow. It is also important to remember that the mount table array entries are not linked, but rather are searched sequentially. The number of mounted file systems should therefore be limited as much as possible.

Summary

While UNIX does allow multiple file systems, each file system which is to be accessed must first be mounted. The mount command allows the system administrator to mount file systems.

When a file system is mounted, a specified directory in a currently mounted file system is specified as the mount point. That directory takes on the root directory of the mounted file system. The inode for the directory on which the new file system is being mounted has a flag set indicating that a file system has been mounted and that inode is referred to as a mounted on inode.

The effect of mounting is to logically join an existing file system with a new file system. The new file system becomes accessible through the root of the existing file system. Information regarding mounts is stored in the mount table.

Points to Ponder

Under what circumstances is it desirable to use the mountable file system feature? Given that file systems on separate physical devices will have slow access, why would you want to mount file systems across devices?

Could any of the the existing file system tables and/or data structures be used in place of the mount table? What modifications would be required to eliminate the mount table? Would there be any advantage to doing so?

11
System Calls to the File System

The previous chapters have explained the file system. They have covered in some detail how the structures and tables of the file system are created, manipulated, and accessed. The interaction and interrelation of the file system tables and structures have also been covered. The most effective method of accessing the file system has been virtually ignored up to now. That method is the use of system calls.

It is the system calls which provide the user with true access to the file system. System calls allow the information contained in the file system to be accessed and modified by user programs (operating, as do all system calls, through the kernel in kernel mode). In support of the system calls are a layer of lower calls, which contain algorithms to do the specific tasks required for the access and manipulation of the file system.

SYSTEM CALL OVERVIEW

System calls are the commands available to the user which request kernel operations. The file system which is in some way impacted indirectly by almost all UNIX operations is directly affected by 19 system calls. These system calls are: open( ), read( ), write( ), lseek( ), close( ), creat( ), mknod( ), chdir( ), chroot( ), chown( ), chmod( ), stat( ), fstat( ), pipe( ), dup( ), mount( ), umount( ), link( ), unlink( ).

It is possible to divide these system calls into seven catagories to facilitate their examination here. These categories are: system calls which return and/or modify file descriptors (pointers to inodes); system calls which assign and free inodes; system calls which set or change file attributes; system calls which do input and or output to or from a process; system calls which change a file system; system calls which cause a change in a process's view of the file system; system calls which use the namei algorithm to parse a path. Figure 11-1 shows the system calls distributed in their seven possible categories.

In this figure several of the system calls appear in more than one category. The namei algorithm (which will be detailed later) is especially important since it supplies the logic that allows the path of a file to be traced in order to locate that file. Despite the fact that these system calls use different logic, accomplish different outcomes and require different input parameters, they share one essential characteristic—all system calls return a -1 to the calling program when they fail. Thus, logic constructed around system calls can use common error handling routines simply by being sensitive to the -1 failure return.

The system calls for the file system must be able to perform two major tasks—they must manipulate files and they must allocate and deallocate buffers. Consistent with UNIX's overall philosophy of reusability, all of the system calls accomplish these tasks with the same underlying algorithms. File system manipulation is accomplished with namei (using iget and iput), falloc, iread, iowait, prele, ialloc, ifree, alloc, free, and bmap. Buffer allocation is performed using getblk, brelse, breadf, breada, and bwrite.

ALGORITHM DEFINITIONS AND LOGIC

The algorithms used by the system calls can be considered as being calls available only to the system calls. Thus, they may be executed only by the kernel and only in kernel mode. If any attempt is made in a user program to execute these algorithms, an error will result. Nevertheless, the structure and calling procedures for invoking these algorithms is the same as that for a system call. Remember, however, that only the system can invoke the algorithms— programmers must gain access to these algorithms through the system calls.

Return File Desc.	Assign Inodes	Set File Attr.	Process Input/ Output	Change File System	Modify View Of File System	Use namei Algorithm	
open	creat	chown	read	mount	chdir	open	creat
close	link	chmod	write	umount	chroot	mknod	chdir
creat	unlink	stat	lseek			chroot	chown
pipe		fstat				chmod	stat
dup						mount	umount

Fig. 11-1. System calls that affect the file system.

namei. The most commonly used algorithm is *namei*. This routine converts the file path name to an inode pointer. The namei routine is invoked from the system calls requiring it to use the following structure:

namei(path, flag)

where:

- ☐ path — the file path to be converted;
- ☐ flag — the type of activity to be performed: seek, create, or delete.

The return from inode is a pointer to a locked inode table entry.

Parsing the path name is an iterative process, so the namei routine is a loop. The first step of this loop is to check to see if the end of the path has been reached. If the routine is at the end of the path and either a matching or empty inode has not been located, an error condition exists and this is returned to the caller. If the end of the path is reached and the component is located, then a pointer to the just-located inode is returned.

The current directory is always searched for an entry matching the current component of the path (thus, if the path is /user/myril/book/chaps/chap1, the current directory will be searched for user, myril, book, chaps, chap1 depending on which component is currently being sought). If the end of the current directory block is reached then the next directory block is retrieved and the new block is searched. If the appropriate inode is located and it is empty, then a pointer to this inode is returned so that the file can be created (assuming that file creation is the desired outcome of the operation). The entire directory is searched until a match for the path name component is located.

Once an entry does match the current path component, it is time to begin the search for the next path component. If the name of the current component is .. (meaning the parent directory) and the current inode is 2 (which is always the root), then the mount table must be searched for a match. This is the condition where a file system has been mounted and a mount point is being crossed. The mount table entries for device and inode (m__dev and m__inodp) are assigned to the current device and inode respectively. Once this assignment has been made the search starts again.

When a match for the current path component is identified, the routines iput( ) and iget( ) are invoked. The iput routine (described in more detail later) replaces the current inode in preparation for getting the newly located inode and cleans up after the use of the current inode. The iget routine (also to be described later) gets the inode for the newly found path component.

Now the path specified is checked and the next component of the path is retrieved. The directory is checked to make sure that permissions exist to read it during the search for a match to the path component, and the search process begins again.

The namei routine always returns either a pointer to the appropriate inode or an error. Note that it does check the mount table so that paths can cross device lines. Note also however, that if a file system is not mounted, then the search will fail because the correct mount table entries will not be present. It is also important to understand that the inode table entry returned by the namei routine is locked when it is returned. This means that the entry should be used and freed as quickly as possible or other processes needing this inode entry will have to wait until it is freed.

iget. The *iget* routine is called by namei to do some of the repetitive tasks involved in returning the pointer to an inode table entry. The structure of the call to iget is:

iget(device, inum)

where:

☐ device — the major and minor device numbers of the inode;
☐ inum — the inode number of the inode to be returned.

The return from iget is a pointer to a locked inode.

During the process of trying to return an inode two conditions can exist: the inode may be in memory or it may be on the disk. If the inode is in memory, then iget will return a pointer to the inode. If the inode is currently locked, iget will sleep until the inode is free. If the inode is on the freelist, it will be removed from the freelist. The inode reference count will be incremented and a pointer to the inode will be returned.

If the inode is not in memory, then it is not currently being used. In this case iget will try to get an inode from the disk-resident inode freelist. If no free inodes are available, an error will be returned. If a free inode is found, then it will be removed from the freelist. The inode number will be reset to an appropriate value (depending on the current system status). The new inode will be placed on the hash queue and initialized. The iget routine will then return a pointer to the inode.

iput. Once an inode has been used, it must be released. The *iput* routine releases an inode and cleans up after its use. The structure of a call to iput is:

iput(inode)

where:

☐ inode — pointer to inode to be released.

The iput routine returns nothing to its caller.

The first step in releasing the inode is to decrement its reference count. If the decremented reference count is zero, then the inode is no longer in active use. If the link count is also zero, then the file disk blocks are freed, the inode mode (i__mode) is set to zero, and the IUPD flag is set to 1 so that the new information will be recorded to disk. Finally, the inode is freed.

Regardless of the link count, if the IUPD flag is set then the inode information is updated to the disk. The inode is released using the prele routine, which will be detailed later. The essence of this routine is that it unlocks the inode. If the reference count is zero, then the inode table slot is put back on the freelist and the i__flag, i__number, and i__count fields are set to zero. If the decremented reference count is not zero, then the prele algorithm is invoked to unlock the inode.

falloc. The *falloc* routine assigns a file descriptor and a file table entry. The calling structure of the falloc routine is:

falloc(inode, request)

where:

☐ inode — inode table entry pointer;
☐ request — request mode.

The return from the falloc routine is a pointer to a file table entry.
First a u__ofile entry is allocated. A file table entry from the freelist is located and the address of that file table entry is placed in the newly allocated u__ofile entry. The *fcount* value in the file table entry is incremented and the inode pointer value is assigned to f__inode. Finally, before returning a pointer to the file table entry, the f__offset field is set to zero and a flag value is assigned to f__flag.

iread. Once a pointer to an inode table entry has been located, the *iread* routine reads an inode into that inode table entry. The calling structure of the iread routine is:

iread(inode)

where:

☐ inode — inode table entry pointer.

The return from iread is a pointer to the given locked inode table entry.
The first step in iread processing is to get the i__list block containing the inode. If an error occurs on this step then the iput routine is used to replace the inode table entry and a null is returned. If no error occurred while retrieving the appropriate i__list block, then the inode structure is copied from the i__list block to the inode table entry. The 3-byte addresses contained in the i__list (di__addr[ ]) are converted to 4-byte addresses (i__addr[ ]). The i__list block is released and a pointer to the inode is returned.

prele. The *prele* routine is invoked to release an inode table entry. This relatively straightforward process has the following calling structure:

    prele(inode)

where:

☐ inode — inode table entry pointer.

There is no return from this routine.

The ILOCK flag for the inode is reset (thus unlocking the inode). If the IWANT flag is set for that inode, indicating that there are processes sleeping and waiting for that inode, then the IWANT flag is reset and wakeup( ) is issued to awaken all processes sleeping on the inode pointer.

ialloc. The *ialloc* routine, which allocates an inode, was discussed in detail in Chapter 9. Its calling structure is:

    ialloc(file__system)

where:

☐ file__system — pointer to file system superblock.

The return from ialloc is a locked inode pointer.

ifree. The *ifree* routine frees an inode. Its operation was detailed in Chapter 9. The calling structure for ifree is:

    ifree(inode)

where:

☐ inode — inode table entry pointer.

There is nothing returned from ifree.

bmap. The *bmap* routine performs the task of computing and retrieving the particular data block for file data retrieval. First impressions aside, this is not a trivial function as the double and triple indirection blocks come into play. The calling structure for bmap is:

    bmap(inode, offset)

where:

☐ inode — pointer to inode table entry
☐ offset — byte offset in file for data being retrieved.

The return from this routine is a pointer to the correct block in the file system, the byte offset into that block, the number of usable bytes in the block and the read ahead block number.

The first step performed by bmap is to calculate the logical block number in the file from the byte offset (that is, the byte offset divided by the BLOCKSIZE). The start byte into that logical block is then determined. The number of bytes to copy is computed and if read ahead is necessary (by virtue of needing data from another block to complete the I/O then the inode for the read ahead is marked. Next, the level of indirection is computed. If the logical block is 10 or less then no indirection is needed. If the logical block is less than BLOCKSIZE divided by four (the number of indirect addresses which could be stored in a block) then only one level of indirection is necessary.

Once the appropriate level of indirection is determined, then the index into the inode or the indirect block appropriate for that level of indirection is computed. The disk block number from the inode or the indirect block at that index is retrieved. If necessary, the buffer from any previous disk read is released (using the brelse algorithm). If there are no more levels of indirection then the block number is returned. If there are more levels, then the next disk block is retrieved, the next appropriate index is computed and the process repeats.

getblk. The *getblk* routine calls the device driver needed to perform a block read from a physical device. The calling structure for getblk is:

getblk(device, block)

where:

☐ device — major and minor device numbers
☐ block — data block number.

The return from the getblk routine is a pointer to the buffer header containing the block.

The first step in the getblk processing is to find the appropriate hash table entry for the requested block. If the block is located in the hash queue, then, if the buffer is busy, sleep and wait for it to be freed, otherwise remove the buffer from the freelist (bfreelist) and return a pointer to the buffer. If there are no free buffers on the hash list, then sleep waiting for any event causing a buffer to become free. The next free buffer will be removed from the freelist and a pointer to it will be returned.

bread. The *bread* routine reads an i__list block into a buffer. The calling structure for bread is:

bread(device, block)

where:

☐ device — major and minor device numbers
☐ block — number of block to be read.

The bread routine first uses getblk to retrieve the system buffer holding the requested block. If the buffer returned has the current version of the block, then a pointer to the buffer is returned. If the buffer retrieved does not have the current version of the block then b__flags is set to READ and b__bcount is set to BLKSIZE. Once the flags are set, the device driver is called to read the block into the buffer. When the I/O is complete, the pointer to the buffer is returned.

brelse. The task of releasing the buffer holding the i__list block is assigned to the *brelse* routine. The calling structure for this routine is:

brelse(buffer)

where:

☐ buffer — pointer to the buffer header.

The brelse routine returns nothing.

If the WANTED flag for the buffer header being released is set then wakeup( ) is issued to awaken all processes sleeping on that buffer header address. If the bfreelist WANTED flag is set on, then wakeup( ) is issued to awaken all processes sleeping on the bfreelist address. If the AGE buffer flag is set, the buffer is placed at the beginning of the bfreelist. Otherwise the buffer is placed at the end of the bfreelist. Finally, the WANTED and BUSY flags are reset.

breada. In order to improve operating efficiency, the kernel tries to anticipate the need for disk reads when processing sequentially through a file. The *breada* function performs the read ahead function. The calling structure for breada is:

breada(block, asblock)

where:

☐ block — file system block number for immediate read
☐ asblock — file system block for asynchronous read.

The return from breada is a pointer to the buffer containing the immediate read block.

If the first block is not in the buffer cache then the buffer for the first block is retrieved using the getblk algorithm. If necessary, a disk read request is initiated to retrieve the correct block. If the second block, that is, the read ahead block, is not available, then a second getblk request is issued. Again, if necessary, a disk read request is issued. At this point a bread is issued to retrieve the pointer to the first buffer. If that first buffer is unavailable, then the process will sleep until it becomes available. Note that the process does not sleep on the second block—because the retrieval of that block is non-critical at this time. The only purpose of retrieving the next block is to have it available when the next step in the controlling process requests that data.

bwrite. The *bwrite* routine writes a disk block. The calling structure for the bwrite routine is:

bwrite(buffer)

where:

☐ buffer — pointer to buffer to be written.

There is no return issued from bwrite.

The bwrite routine immediately issues a disk write request. If the I/O is synchronous (meaning that it must be completed before the process can continue) then bwrite will sleep until the I/O is complete and then release the buffer (using brelse). Otherwise the buffer is marked for a delayed awrite and marked to be put at the head of the freelist.

SYSTEM CALL DEFINITION AND LOGIC

The system calls which operate on and with the file system rely heavily on the previously defined algorithms. In this section the logic for each of the system calls will be briefly described. Because the invocation structure for the system calls has, in many cases, been presented elsewhere and is summarized in Appendix A, the detailed invocation for each call will not be presented here. Instead, the key logical steps involved in making the system calls work are briefly presented. The order of the calls in this section is as shown in Fig. 11-2.

open( ). The *open( )* system call opens a file and returns the file descriptor for that file. First, open( ) invokes namei to convert the file name to an inode. If the file does not exist or if access is not permitted, an error is returned. A file table entry for the inode is allocated and initialized. If the file open specifies that the file is to be truncated (an open type of create), then free is invoked to free the file blocks. The inode, which was locked by namei is unlocked and the user file descriptor is returned.

read( ). The *read( )* system call reads a specified amount of data from a user file and returns a count of the amount of data read. First, the file table entry indicated by the ffile descriptor is retrieved. The file accessibility

```
System_Calls_Accessing_Existing_Files
open()
read()
write()
lseek()
close()


System_Calls_Which_Create_New_Files
creat()
mknod()


System_Calls_Which_Maneuver_Through_The_File_System
chdir()
chroot()
chown()
chmod()
stat()
fstat()


Advanced_System_Calls
pipe()
dup()
mount()
umount()
link()
unlink()
```

Fig. 11-2. System call order.

(permission) is checked. The parameters in the user area are set to indicate the address to which the read data is to be returned, the byte count or the amount of data to be read, and a flag is set indicating that the user has I/O in progress. The inode for the file is retrieved and locked. The byte offset in the user area is set based on the file table offset field.

Using the bmap routine, the file offset is converted to a disk block. The offset into the file is computed and the number of bytes to read is determined. If there are no bytes available to be read then the read call is considered to be complete since the end of the file has been reached. Otherwise the block of data is read using either bread or breada (depending on whether or not read ahead is required). The data block is copied from the system buffer to the user address. The user area fields are updated to indicate that the read has occurred and the buffer is released. This process is repeated until the required number of bytes have been read.

When the read is complete, the inode is unlocked, the file table offset is updated so that it will be accurate for the next read, and the number of bytes read is returned to the caller. Note that whenever the number of bytes read does not equal the number of bytes requested, the end of the file has been reached during the read.

write( ). When data needs to be written to disk, the *write( )* system call is used. Similar to the read( ) call, the write( ) system call writes a specified number of bytes to the disk and returns a count of the number of bytes actually written.

The logic for the write( ) call is virtually identical to that of read with the following exception. If there is no corresponding block for the file offset to be written, then alloc is invoked to create a new block. The data to be written is then placed in that block. If for any reason the number of bytes actually written does not correspond to the number of bytes requested to be written, then a severe error has occurred and write( ) returns an error.

lseek( ). The judicious use of the *lseek( )* system call allows random access to a file by manipulating the file offset field. The only processing required for this system call is the retrieval of the correct file table entry and the adjustment of the file table offset. The read( ) and write( ) calls will then use the adjusted offset as their new read or write starting positions.

close( ). The *close( )* system call closes an open file identified by a file descriptor. The key function performed by close is the decrementing of the file table reference count. If this count is greater than one, then all that is necessary is that it be decremented and the close is complete. If the count is one, so that decremented it is zero, then the file table entry is freed and the in-core inode is released using iput.

creat( ). The *creat( )* system call causes a new file to be created. The creat( ) call makes a new file in the file system and returns a file descriptor for that file.

First, the inode for the file name must be retrieved using namei. If the file already exists and access to it is not permitted then the inode is released using iput and an error is returned. If the file does not exist then ialloc is invoked to assign a free inode from the file system. A new directory entry is created in the parent directory for the newly created file. A file table entry is initialized for the inode. If the file already existed when the creat( ) was issued, then free is invoked to free the file blocks. Finally the inode is unlocked and the file descriptor is returned to the caller.

mknod( ). Just as creat( ) is used to create regular files, the *mknod( )* system call is used to create special files. In this case special files include named pipes, device files and directories. The mknod( ) call creates a file with a specified name, type and permission set on a particular device. It does not return anything but does leave a new directory entry.

Only the superuser can create device files and directories, so if the user is not the superuser and the request is not for a named pipe to be created then an error is returned. The namei routine is used to get the inode for the parent of the file about to be created. If the specified file already exists then the inode of the parent is released using iput and an error is returned. The ialloc routine is invoked to assign a free inode from the file system to the new file. A new directory entry is created in the parent directory. The parent directory inode is released with iput. If the new file is a block or character special file then the major and minor device numbers are written into the inode structure. Finally, the inode for the new file is released with the iput routine.

chdir( ). The *chdir( )* system call changes the current or working directory for a process. This system call takes the new pathname as input and returns nothing.

As with many of the previous system calls, namei is invoked to get an inode—this time the inode for the new directory name. If the inode returned is not that of a directory, or if permissions do not exist allowing access to that directory, then the inode is released (iput) and an error is returned. If the inode is valid then it is unlocked, the inode for the current directory is released (iput) and the inode for the new directory is placed in the appropriate field of the user area.

chroot( ). The *chroot( )* system call allows a new effective root directory for a process to be specified. The actual root directory (/) is stored in a global variable and will not be changed, but the chroot( ) call allows a new effective root for the process to be stored in the user area. This call follows exactly the same logic as chdir( ) except that instead of changing the current directory in the user area, it changes the root directory. The impact of this change is that whenever namei is invoked for the calling process, it will search for the named file using the newly specified directory as the root rather than the actual root directory(/).

chown( ) and chmod( ). The *chown( )* system call allows the owner of a file to be changed. The *chmod( )* system call allows the permissions associated with a file to be changed. The logic for both of these calls is virtually identical and equally simple. The file name is converted to an inode with the namei routine. If the caller has the permission to make the requested changes then either the owner or mode fields in the inode are changed and the inode is released (using iput).

stat( ) and fstat( ). These system calls, *stat( )* and *fstat( )*, return file status information. They allow a process to determine almost any status information about a file including file type, owner, permissions, file size, number of links, the inode number and the file access times. The only difference between stat( ) and fstat( ) is that fstat( ) requires a file descriptor, while stat( ) needs only the file name. Thus, the first step in stat( ) is the invocation of namei to get the appropriate inode, while fstat( ) can determine the inode form of the file table entry.

Once the inode is known, iget is used to return a pointer to the inode table entry. The iread routine reads the inode into the inode table entry. The i_list block is read into the buffer using bread. If I/O is needed, then getblk is invoked. Once the necessary data blocks have been retrieved and loaded, brelse is used to replace the buffer with the i_list block. The status data is copied to the user space, iput releases the inode and prele is used to release the inode table entry.

pipe( ). Pipes are created using the *pipe( )* system call. This call takes as input a pointer to an array which will contain the file descriptors for reading and writing the new pipe. The call completes this array by assigning the read and the write file descriptors.

The first step for pipe( ) is to assign a new inode for the pipe using the ialloc routine. Two file table entries are allocated: one for reading and one for writing. The file table entries are initialized to point to the new inode. File table descriptors are allocated, again one for reading and one for writing and they are initialized to point to the appropriate file table entries. The inode reference count is set to 2 and the inode reader and writer count is initialized to one.

dup( ). The *dup( )* system call simply copies a file descriptor and returns a new file descriptor, thus providing a second descriptor for an existing file. All this call does is copy a file descriptor into the first free slot of the user file descriptor table and return a new file descriptor. Since the file descriptor is duplicated, the reference count of the file table entry is incremented.

mount( ). The *mount( )* system call allows a new file system to be incorporated in the hierarchy of an existing file system. The mount( ) call uses the name of the device to be mounted and the directory to be mounted on. Except for error conditions, there are no returns from the mount( ) call.

Only a superuser can execute the mount command, so if the caller is not the superuser an error is returned immediately. Assuming that the superuser is the caller, an inode is obtained for the device to be mounted using namei. An inode for the directory to be mounted on is obtained in similar fashion. If the directory to be mounted on is not a directory, or if the reference count of its inode is greater than one the inodes are released (with iput) and an error is returned.

An empty slot in the mount table is then located. A free block is obtained and the superblock of the system being mounted is read into that block and the superblock fields are initialized. The iget routine is used to get the root inode of the file system being mounted and it is then saved in the mount table. The mounted on directory is so marked and the inodes are released and unlocked.

umount( ). The *umount( )* system call causes a mounted file system to be unmounted, thus separating the file system from the hierarchy of the mounted on file system. Once unmounted, the file system is no longer accessible.

As with mount( ), only a superuser can perform a umount( ) call. If the user is not a superuser, an error is returned immediately. The inode of the special file (the device containing the mounted file system) is obtained with namei. The major and minor device numbers of the file system being unmounted are determined. The inode of the special file is released using iput. The superblock for the file system being dismounted is updated as are its inodes. The file system's buffers are flushed. If any of the file system files are still in use an error is returned.

The root inode of the mounted file system is obtained from the file system and that inode is locked. The inode is released with iput and close( ) is issued for the special device. Any buffers in the buffer pool belonging to the dismounted file system are removed. The inode of the mounted on directory is obtained from the mount table and is locked. The flag identifying the directory as mounted on is cleared and the inode is released (iput). The buffer used for the superblock is freed and the mount table slot is freed.

link.( ) The *link( )* system call is used to link a file with a new file name. The impact of a link is to create a new directory entry for an existing inode. The link( ) call simply takes the current file name and allows a new file name to be associated with it.

First, namei is used to derive the inode for the existing file. If there are too many links on the file, or if a directory is being linked without permission of the superuser, then an error is returned after the inode is released. The link count for the inode is incremented. The disk copy of the inode is updated and the inode is unlocked. The inode of the parent directory that is to contain the new file name is obtained by namei. If the new file name already exists, then the preceding updates are reversed, the inode is released and an error is returned. A new directory entry is created in the parent directory of the new file. Finally, the parent directory and the existing file inodes are released.

unlink( ). The *unlink( )* system call reverses a link( ) call and removes a directory entry for a file. The unlink( ) call unlinks or removes the directory entry for the file name specified.

The parent inode of the file to be retrieved is obtained using namei. If the current directory is being unlinked, then the inode reference count is incremented. If the file being unlinked is not the current directory, then the inode of the file being unlinked is retrieved through use of namei. Only the superuser can unlink a directory, so if the file is a directory and the user is not a superuser, the inodes are released and an error is returned. The inode number of the unlinked file is zeroed and the parent directory is updated. The inode of the parent directory is released. The file link count is decremented and the file inode is released. The iput routine checks to see if the link count for an inode is zero and if it is, frees the file blocks using free, and frees the inode using ifree.

OF INTEREST TO PROGRAMMERS

This chapter has outlined the function and logic of the system calls impacting the file system. Programmers should be aware of the capabilities and limitations of these system calls and use them appropriately. In addition, understanding of the logical processes involved in performing these system calls will sensitize the programmer to their impact on overall system performance.

Summary

System calls to the file system provide the programmer with access to the power of the kernel. Programmers use the system calls to ask the kernel to perform functions on their behalf. The system calls themselves make calls to lower level algorithms (such as namei).

Points to Ponder

What is the purpose for having system calls which request kernel functions? Why not allow direct programmer access to the kernel?

What is the impact of making a system call on the performance of a process? Is there any way to organize system calls within a program to optimize performance?

Basic UNIX
Input and Output

UNIX input and output, referred to as UNIX I/O, is the transfer of data between a UNIX process and an I/O device. The traditional I/O devices for UNIX systems are disk drives, tape drives, screens (monitors), keyboards, printers and the like. When an executing process requires data from an I/O device, or when it needs to write information to an I/O device, the operating system has the task of correctly and efficiently routing the data. The data is passed between the I/O area of the user address space and the I/O device buffers. Often the data is passed through an intermediate set of buffers.

When I/O is in progress, three types of data are being passed. First the data itself is passed between the process and the I/O device. But the data alone is not sufficient information for successful I/O. In addition to the data, control information must be passed. This information is written or set by the process and read by the system. It consists of information such as the source/destination address and the amount of data to be transferred in terms of bytes or blocks. Finally, the status information is read by the process and set by the system. This information reflects the state of the I/O operation, telling us whether it is in progress, waiting, complete, or in some other condition.

The single most important feature of all UNIX I/O is that it is interrupt driven. The process requests I/O, and the operating system initiates it, but ultimately I/O is controlled via *device interrupts*. The operating system is informed of I/O completion via a *completion interrupt*. When the interrupt is received, it is serviced as is necessary. Any processes sleeping on that interrupt are awakened and any control bytes are updated.

The goal of the operating system during I/O is to map the device data area (that buffer containing the device data) to the system address space of the process image (that is, the I/O data area for the process). During this mapping, the control/status data area for the device is also mapped to the control/status data area for the process.

There are two types of I/O in the UNIX operating system—buffered and unbuffered. Buffered I/O passes through a set of system buffers and will be described shortly. Unbuffered I/O uses the *direct memory access* (DMA) facility to directly transfer data between the process I/O area and the device. No kernel buffers are used when the DMA facility is used. Disk I/O is frequently unbuffered since the disk is a relatively fast device. One of the key factors in determining the viability of using the DMA facility is the speed of the I/O device. A slow I/O device is not generally a good candidate for DMA because in that situation, DMA would slow down all system operations while I/O takes place.

INPUT/OUTPUT BUFFERING

Buffers are intermediate holding areas in the kernel space used to store data in transit from an I/O device to process memory. It is important to understand that it makes no difference whatsoever to the device whether it is being buffered or not. Just as the kernel ensures that processes see all data from the I/O device as a data stream, all I/O devices simply see and send data with no concern for destination.

Why is it ever necessary to buffer data? Buffering can improve system performance and efficiency in several instances. First, buffering can reduce the amount of process switching by collecting bytes until a sufficient number of bytes has been collected. By collecting bytes in this fashion, it is not necessary to switch to or from the process as each byte is processed.

Another benefit of buffering is the storage of unwanted units of I/O. Some I/O devices require or provide blocks as opposed to bytes of data. Buffers can be used to hold the unneeded data until it is needed. The minimal unit of processing for a process is one byte. Some devices require a minimum of a block (1024k bytes in most cases) of data before data can be written to or read from them. The buffer can hold this additional data, or serve as a storage area until sufficient data has been collected.

Some devices require that data transformation occur before data can be read from or written to the devices. For example, terminals require that delay characters be inserted before providing data to processes. Buffers can be used to store the data as the data transforms are being performed.

All processes are not always ready for the data as it comes from a device. A process may not be prepared to receive the data from a keyboard. A buffer is used to collect the data until the process is ready to begin processing it. Conversely, the device may be in use and not ready to accept data from a process. The buffer serves as a holding area for the data until the device is ready to receive it.

132

The UNIX operating system provides two types of buffers—the *system buffer caches* and *character queues*. The system buffer caches are a set of buffers in the kernel space which store data. These buffers are reusable and are very high speed. Buffer caching provides a form of random access to the data in the buffers. Character queues are non-reusable, low speed, non-random access buffer areas. Each of these buffers has its place in the UNIX environment as will be shown.

SYSTEM BUFFER CACHES

Data is transferred to the system buffer caches between the process I/O area and the I/O device. When the buffer caches are used for I/O, the data as well as the control and status information is maintained in these buffer caches. The data transfer between the buffer cache and the process always occurs via the DMA facility. The buffer caches are memory themselves, just as the process I/O area is memory, so the DMA facility is used in this case to perform a memory to memory copy.

When using the buffer caches, read operations do not necessarily perform physical reads. If the data required can be found in the buffer caches then it is retrieved from these caches without ever activating the I/O device. Similarly, write operations do not necessarily perform physical writes. Instead, when the buffering is in use, the data will be written to a buffer or buffers. The used buffers will be marked as dirty and when all the buffers are dirty, the entire cache will be written to disk. Thus, with buffer caches, physical I/O is necessary only when the memory buffers are exhausted.

One note of importance is that buffer caching does not eliminate any of the control or status information. This information is recorded in its own area of the buffer caches.

CHARACTER QUEUES

While it makes sense for block-oriented devices such as disk drives to use buffer caching, a different type of buffering is more reasonable for character-oriented devices such as keyboards and terminals. Character queues provide the buffering for character-oriented devices. In this capacity, character queues also use the same control and status mechanisms as buffer caches. The difference between character queues and buffer caches is the manner in which they are read and written.

A character queue is either written by the I/O device and read by the process or written by the process and read by the device. In either case the reading occurs at relatively low speeds, one character at a time. Furthermore, while buffer caches can be read many times, character queues may be read only once. As each character is read, it is effectively destroyed. Character buffers cannot be reused.

INPUT/OUTPUT DEVICES AND DEVICE DRIVERS

There are six distinct types of devices recognized by UNIX and these devices use their own types of buffering. The devices are:

- ☐ disk drives
- ☐ tape drives
- ☐ terminals
- ☐ communication lines
- ☐ printers
- ☐ artificial devices

Disk drives are fairly fast devices and are of course heavily used by UNIX processes. The disk drives tend to use either the system buffer caches or unbuffered I/O. (Often products such as database management systems will advertise as providing both buffered or raw I/O. This is a reference to using the system buffer caches or the unbuffered I/O.) Tape drives provide much the same functionality as do disk drives and use similar buffering capabilities.

Terminals are character-oriented devices. When typing is going on, a relatively long time can pass between keystrokes and similarly long times can pass between delivery of characters to the screen. Terminals tend to use character queues.

The very nature of communication lines requires that characters come in singly over the lines and then require serial processing. This makes character queues a natural medium for communication lines.

Printers will use character queues or unbuffered I/O depending on the characteristics of the specific printer. Extremely slow printers will generally use character queues whereas high-speed printers generally use unbuffered I/O. There is nothing to preclude a printer from using the buffer caches, but such a use is wasteful since data going to a printer is never going to be reused—a primary consideration in the employment of buffer caches.

Finally, the artificial devices are memory itself, the null device and other system use-oriented devices. Memory to memory transfers are unbuffered. The null device does no I/O at all. The other artificial devices are generally unbuffered, but the appropriate techniques will vary based on the actual use of the device.

Whatever the technique used to perform I/O between a process and an I/O device, the actual interface between the operating system, the process and the device is handled by means of software called a *device driver*. When a process requests I/O, the operating system activates the appropriate device driver for the process through a kernel-level process. This may be caused by calls such as read or write. This invocation and activation of a device driver starts the I/O process. As soon as the device driver has been notified of the request, the calling process resumes control—but the I/O may not yet be complete.

When the I/O is complete, the device signals that completion via an interrupt. The device driver is sensitive to that interrupt and in turn signals completion to the kernel and the invoking process.

Thus, device driver routines are split over two levels. The base level of a device driver is executed synchronously on a call from a process and immediately returns control to the process. Any waiting for completion is a function of an operating system determination and is not controlled by the device driver. The interrupt level of the device driver determines which routines get executed when interrupts are sent from the device. The interrupt level is executed asynchronously from the point of view of the process that invoked the device driver. This is because interrupts come whenever the device needs to update status and not at any particular point in the processing.

Device tables provide the interface between the device drivers and the operating system. There are two device tables for the UNIX operating system—the *block device switch table (bdevsw)* and the *character device switch table (cdevsw)*. The block device switch table contains pointers to drivers for all the devices using buffer caches. The character device switch table contains pointers to all the devices using either character buffers or unbuffered I/O. The major device number is used as the index into the appropriate switch table for a device.

Since the device driver is an independent process, UNIX provides two mechanisms for user I/O. When unbuffered I/O is underway, the I/O area of the user process must be locked in memory—it cannot be swapped out while I/O is underway. When buffer caching is being used, as soon as the device driver is called, the swappable image of the process can be swapped out. The I/O process will continue loading the buffer cache until the process is swapped back in and can begin processing the data.

DETAILS OF THE SYSTEM BUFFER CACHE

The system buffer caches provide two major benefits to the UNIX operating system. First, they store data in a holding area between the device and the process. Since device I/O is asynchronous and process I/O is synchronous, the buffers serve as a shield to the process and provide a steady and consistent view of the data without regard to timing considerations. Second, as much data as possible is held in the buffers as long as possible. Thus, reads and writes to physical devices are kept to a minimum. This caching effect provides a more efficient use of system resources.

All of the I/O control and status data is retained in the buffer headers. Figure 12-1 shows the key data elements of the buffer header structure. Note that buffer headers are used even during unbuffered I/O to hold the control and status information for that I/O process.

Figure 12-2 lists the possible status flags which can be indicated in the B_flags field. Note that these are not necessarily exclusive conditions and that more than one condition can exist simultaneously.

Of all the fields in the buffer, only five are directly necessary for the performance of I/O. First, the address of the data area in memory stored in b_un is required. Additionally, the device on which the I/O is performed (b_dev) is derived from the inode table. The address of the data area on the device is in b_blkno. The amount of I/O in bytes is stored in b_count. Finally, the b_flag field is required so that the precise status of the operation can be determined.

The b_error field indicates what type of error occurred during the I/O and is eventually transferred to the user area. The impact of the error in terms

b_flags	Status flags
b_forw	Management link
b_back	Management link
av_forw	Management link
av_back	Management link
b_dev	Device number of data block
b_count	Number of bytes of I/O
b_un	Pointer to I/O data
b_blkno	Block number on device
b_error	I/O error code
b_resid	Number of bytes remaining due to error
b_start	I/O start time
b_proc	Pointer to process table entry involved in I/O

Fig. 12-1. Data elements of the buffer header structure.

of bytes of I/O remaining is stored in the b_resid field (this is the residual bytes field). The start time for I/O stored in b_start is used to measure device response time by the system accounting functions. The process table pointer stored in b_proc is only used during swapping or if the process must be locked in memory because unbuffered I/O is taking place.

The four management link members (av_forw, av_back, b_forw, b_back) are used to maintain the buffer cache lists. The buffers in the buffer cache can be part of one or more of the following lists: available list, device list, or driver I/O queue. The available list maintains the list of all buffers available for allocation. This is a doubly-linked list using av_forw and av_back. It is headed by a buffer header with no corresponding buffer called bfreelist. Any non-busy buffer (B_BUSY not on) is linked to this list.

The buffer structure associated with bfreelist contains information needed to maintain the available list. In particular, the b_count field contains the

B_WRITE	Write buffer when I/O begins
B_READ	Read buffer when I/O begins
B_DONE	I/O complete
B_ASYNC	Asynchronous write
B_DELWRI	Buffer dirty; write as soon as possible
B_AGE	Move buffer to beginning of available list
B_STALE	Information in buffer is invalid
B_ERROR	Error occurred during I/O
B_BUSY	Buffer in use
B_WANTED	Buffer sought for allocation'
B_PHYS	Header in use undergoing unbuffered I/O

Fig. 12-2. Status flags in the b-flags field.

136

number of available buffers. If a process requires a buffer, but the count is zero, the B_WANTED flag is set in all the buffers and the process needing the buffer sleeps. As soon as a buffer is released it is linked into the available list, the B_WANTED flag is turned off and all processes sleeping on a free buffer are awakened.

The device list contains the list of all buffers currently associated with each device. This is also a doubly-linked list using b_forw and b_back. The list is headed by an entry in the buffer hash table. The exact hash entry is determined by hashing the device number with the specific block number to determine the hash index. The specific buffer is determined by matching the b_dev and b_blkno entries.

Finally, the driver I/O queue contains the list of buffers that are actually undergoing or waiting for I/O on a particular device. Each device driver I/O queue is a singly-linked list of buffer headers. The buffer headers are linked via the av_forw field. Each device has a driver I/O queue header which maintains the pointers to the buffers awaiting I/O.

The system buffer cache structures provide each device, driver and process with fast access to memory buffers. These buffers are managed and maintained on their lists as are the other buffer lists throughout the UNIX system.

DETAILS OF THE CHARACTER QUEUE

Character devices are not well served by the buffer-caching mechanisms and have therefore been provided with a mechanism of their own. While the character mechanism does not provide the reusability of the system buffering, it is much simpler and does provide straightforward buffering for character-oriented devices.

The basic organization of the character buffer is the cblock. A cblock structure has the data fields shown in Fig. 12-3.

The c_data array is an array of *CLSIZE* size. CLSIZE is a parameter which can be set or tuned by the system administrator and determines the size of the character buffers. A normal value for CLSIZE is 64 (indicating character buffers of 64 characters).

The cblock structures are headed by and organized into clist structures. Every character device has one or more clists. The fields in a clist are:

c_cc   Total number of characters in the clist.
c_cf   Pointer to first cblock in clist.
c_cl   Pointer to last cblock in clist.

c_next	Pointer to next cblock
c_first	Index into c_data array of next character to be read
c_last	Index into c_data array of next character to be written
c_data	Array of fixed but tunable size of characters

Fig. 12-3. cblock data fields.

Just as the buffer caches are organized into free- or in-use lists, the cblocks are always either on a cfreelist or part of a clist. The free cblocks are headed by a structure called chead which contains information about the freelist. The chead structure contains:

c__next	Pointer to next available cblock.
c__size	Always CLSIZE.
c__flag	Any non-zero value indicates a process is sleeping for a cblock.

When the system is initialized, all the cblocks are placed on the freelist. Just as the size of a cblock is adjustable, the total number of cblocks is adjustable. The system value *NCLIST* contains the maximum number of cblocks.

In general the operation of the character buffers is very simple. Whenever the getc or putc operations (or equivalent kernel-level single-character operations) are performed, the clist or clists for the appropriate device are loaded. When a getc is performed, the first cblock in the clist with data is read using the index in c__first (first character to be read) for that cblock. The c__first counter is incremented and the c__cc (total characters in the clist) field is decremented. Conversely, when a putc is performed, the c__last field is decremented and the c__cc field is incremented.

Note that the characters can only be read or written one time. These are not reusable buffer areas. Any process reading data from these buffers is responsible for storing that data or it will be irretrievably lost.

OF INTEREST TO PROGRAMMERS

The primary concern for programmers in this area of UNIX is choosing the correct buffering mechanism for most efficient I/O. In some cases the choice is already made, since drivers are not provided for all approaches for all devices. It is always possible to write a device driver and provide a currently unavailable buffering technique for any device.

Unbuffered I/O will always be the fastest for the particular process involved. Any process involved in unbuffered I/O is locked into memory and cannot be swapped out. This will have a negative impact on overall system performance however. First, there will be less memory available for other processes to swap in and out. Second, the I/O device will be tied up with the particular process for very long intervals making it unavailable to other processes. Therefore, unbuffered I/O should be used only with high-speed devices such as disk drives and memory and then only in well-monitored environments.

System buffer caches provide the fairest approach to I/O from a system view. Using buffer caches ensures the fewest physical reads and writes and optimizes the I/O process. Processes waiting for I/O that are using buffer caches can be swapped. The negative side to buffer caching is that while the buffers are written, they are not immediately recorded on the disk. Should there be a system crash, those unrecorded buffers would be lost. When dealing with very sensitive data, care should be taken to ensure that not too much data is retained unrecorded in the caches.

Character buffers are generally only appropriate for low-speed character-oriented devices. Since considerable processing is required for each character, the speed of character buffers will always be relatively slow. Additionally, since the buffers are not reusable, caution should be used to ensure that important data is recorded elsewhere. This approach is sound for low-speed character-oriented devices such as keyboards.

Summary

The transfer of data between devices such as terminals, printers, disk drives, tape drives, etc. is referred to as UNIX I/O. When I/O is in progress, three types of information are passed—the data, control information and status information.

All UNIX I/O is interrupt driven. Two types of interrupts signal the status of the I/O. The device interrupt signals that the device is in the process of performing I/O. The completion interrupt signals that the I/O is complete. Remember that processes will sleep and/or wake on the basis of these interrupts.

I/O in the UNIX environment can be either buffered or unbuffered. Buffered I/O goes to/from a device through an intermediate memory buffer. Unbuffered I/O goes directly between the process data space and the device. Buffering is somewhat slower but more controlled than unbuffered I/O. Unbuffered I/O is much faster for fast devices but causes great performance degradation when used with slow devices.

Two types of buffers may be involved in I/O. The system buffer is reusable kernel space. This buffer cache is usually involved with fast block oriented devices. Slower character oriented devices use the character queue. The character queue is non-reusable in the sense that once data has been read from it the data is gone from it. Character queues are very low speed.

All I/O is processed through device drivers. The device drivers are software modules which handle the formatting and control of data as it passes to and from the device.

Points to Ponder

It would have been possible to design UNIX with non-interrupt driven I/O. Such a design would have entailed some type of device polling. What would the assets of such a design have been? What about liabilities?

Are there any cases where it would be desirable to use the system buffer cache for character oriented devices? Conversely, would it ever be desirable to process block devices through the character queues?

Non-buffered input with slow devices causes a degradation in system performance. Is there any technique which could be developed using either interprocess communication or special device drivers which would help improve the performance of unbuffered input even when used with a slow device?

13

UNIX Terminal Input and Output

The general approach to UNIX input and output was described in the previous chapter. Terminal I/O is not different in philosophy, but does receive some special consideration through special kernel software. Terminal I/O is different because the terminal is the user interface with the UNIX operating system. As such, it must be somewhat more responsive and sensitive to human considerations while maintaining efficiency regarding the hardware and software interface.

The basic difference between terminal I/O and other forms of I/O is a collection of special software modules called *line discipline modules*. These special modules interface with the terminal device drivers. Line discipline modules provide the special case-handling and interpretive capabilities required by the terminal.

Terminal I/O provides two distinct modes of input and output. These modes are referred to as *canonical* (or "cooked") and *raw*. In canonical mode, the line discipline modules convert the raw data to canonical data—which is the input that the user really meant. Canonical data processes the destructive backspaces (erasures), line deletes, and tab expansions etcetera before sending the data from the terminal to the process or from the process to the terminal. Thus, in canonical mode, the user only needs to be concerned with the traditional corrected and expanded view of the data.

In raw mode, the line discipline modules pass the data from the process to the terminal to the process without any conversion whatsoever. The process is responsible for handling any type of special characters and data parsing.

The line discipline modules provide many capabilities and functions. They parse input strings into lines based on carriage return characters. They process the erase characters. Lines can be deleted with a single kill character via the line discipline modules. Characters received at the terminal are echoed to the terminal. Special characters such as tabs are processed and expanded by the line discipline modules. Special situations such as terminal disconnects (hangups), communication line drops, and delete key (logoff) have their signals generated by the line discipline modules. Finally, line discipline modules allow raw mode processing. These capabilities are summarized in Fig. 13-1.

CANONICAL MODE TERMINAL DRIVER

Terminal I/O drivers have three clists associated with them. One of these clists stores data for output to the terminal, another stores the raw data as it is input or received from the terminal, and the third stores the "cooked" or canonical input data after it has been processed by the line discipline modules.

When a process writes to a terminal, the terminal driver immediately invokes the line discipline modules. The line discipline module loop processes each character of output from the process user data space and, after processing, places it on the output clist. An example of the processing that takes place in this direction is the expansion of tabs from one special control character to a series of spaces.

The physical I/O from a clist is triggered when a *high water mark* is hit. In other words, the data from a clist is not physically written until a certain preset amount of data is on the clist. The high water mark is encountered before the clist is full, however, since typically the physical I/O will be slower than the loading of data to the clist. Thus, the physical unloading of the clist will begin while there is still some amount of space in the clist. This method of use of the clists provides minimal risk of causing a process to sleep because the clist is full.

In order to prevent unnecessary physical writes, the clist also has a *low water mark*. Once the amount of data in the clist drops below this low water mark, processing will cease until the high water mark is again encountered, or until the process signals that it is entirely finished writing data.

```
Line Discipline Functions

   -- Parse Input Strings To Lines
   -- Process Erase Characters
   -- Process Kill Characters To Delete Lines
   -- Echo Received Characters To Terminal
   -- Expand Output
   -- Generate Terminal Condition Signals
   -- Process Raw Mode
```

Fig. 13-1. Line discipline functions.

When the clist for terminal output hits its high water mark, the line discipline module calls the terminal driver process to transmit data to the terminal. As the transmission is going on the writing process is put to sleep.

When the clist is emptied to below its low water mark, an interrupt is generated. At this time, processes sleeping on the event, now that the terminal can accept data, are awakened. When the process has no more user area data to send to the terminal, the line discipline modules call the terminal driver to transmit all remaining data to the terminal.

It is possible for multiple processes to write to the same terminal. In this case the output from each process will be sent to the terminal as required by the terminal driver and the line discipline modules. At the terminal the data may well appear garbled unless the processes synchronize the data to the terminal.

Reading data in canonical mode is somewhat more complex than writing to the terminal. When a read( ) call is issued, it specifies the number of bytes to read. The line discipline modules cause the read( ) to be satisfied as soon as a carriage return is encountered, even if the character count is not satisfied.

The reading process will issue its read( ) call and sleep until a line of data is sent. As data is entered at the terminal, the terminal interrupt handler invokes the line discipline modules to place the data being entered in two places. First, the data is placed on the raw input clist, and it is also immediately placed on the output clist for immediate echo back to the terminal.

As soon as a carriage return character is encountered, an interrupt is generated to awaken all processes sleeping on the receipt of a line of data. The read( ) process causes the line discipline modules to run and remove the characters from the raw clist. As the characters are removed, all erase and kill processing is done and the characters are placed on the canonical clist. Finally, the characters are copied to the user data space until either a carriage return is encountered or until the count specified in the read is satisfied.

The special case of the Ctrl-d character (signifying end of file) is processed by the line discipline modules. When this character is encountered, all data sent to that point is processed, up to but not including the Ctrl-d, and the read is terminated.

Note that all of this processing is based on the use of "dumb" terminals. "Intelligent" terminals, which are becoming increasingly common, are able to "cook" their own data without using any of the CPU processing. The basic handling of terminals is still the same for the UNIX operating system, whether the terminal is intelligent or dumb, but the amount of CPU processing required is less when intelligent terminals are used.

RAW MODE TERMINAL DRIVERS

The ioctl( ) system call is used to set terminal parameters. Among the terminal parameters which can be set by this call is the type of line discipline to use. Processes can set terminals into raw mode with the ioctl( ) call. Processing in the raw mode is the picture of simplicity.

In raw mode, the line discipline modules transmit the characters exactly as they are entered with no input processing of any type. The carriage return character has no special meaning in raw mode and is treated as any other character. A read( ) call is satisfied either after a minimum number of characters has been input or after a specified period of time has elapsed between characters being entered. The amount of time is determined by another parameter which can be specified by the ioctl( ) call.

The processing of the characters entered follows exactly the same pattern as in canonical mode. The characters are immediately placed in the raw clist. When the read( ) is satisfied, the characters are transferred from the raw clist to the canonical clist with no character translation or interpretation. The characters are then moved from the canonical queue to the user process I/O space in the same manner as occurs in the canonical read.

OF INTEREST TO PROGRAMMERS

Two aspects of terminal I/O processing and I/O processing in general are of interest to programmers. First, the programmer must be aware of when to use canonical mode versus when to use raw mode. Second, the details of the ioctl( ) system call are useful to know.

Generally speaking, canonical mode is best for simple terminal I/O. It allows the special characters to be handled transparently to the program and allows the output to be processed as is normally expected. For sophisticated I/O processing, the raw mode may be necessary. Word processing and text editing applications require raw mode since the programmer must be in control of carriage return characters. Also, in general, raw mode processing will be faster than cooked processing, since there is relatively less processing to be done.

The ioctl( ) system call itself is quite simple and quite general. It can be used to perform a large number of functions on devices, which in most cases will be special file character type devices. The call to ioctl( ) is:

```
int       fildes,        /* open file descriptor */
          request;       /* device dependent function to be performed */

int       ioctl(fildes, request, arg);
```

In this call arg is specific to the device and request. When used with a terminal device (/dev/tty*), the file descriptor works in conjunction with the termio.h include file. The default values for erase and kill characters, baud rate, line discipline and processing types are contained in the the termio.h file. Note that ioctl( ) can be used to modify the setting for devices other than terminals.

Summary

Terminal I/O is philosophically the same as all other UNIX I/O. It must, however, receive some special handling since it performs the actual man-machine interface. The special handling aspect of the terminal I/O is found in the line discipline modules. These modules interface with the terminal device drivers and provide the special case handling (such as Ctrl-d processing) and interpretive capabilities required of a terminal.

Terminal I/O has two modes—canonical or cooked and raw. Canonical mode provides the processing of backspaces, tabs and special characters. Raw mode accepts and displays data in a WYSIWYG (what you see is what you get) mode.

Data to and from the terminal is processed through three character lists or clists. One clist stores data for output to a terminal. Another clist stores the raw input. The third clist stores data as it is cooked from the raw input clist.

Points to Ponder

What is the advantage of having special line discipline modules? Why not just write more sophisticated terminal device drivers?

When is it appropriate to use the canonical form of the data? When is it inappropriate?

UNIX Initialization and Termination

What goes on when a UNIX system is booted or initialized, and how does the UNIX system behave when it is brought down or terminated? These are the topics under discussion in this chapter.

As with all operating systems, UNIX begins when its bootstrap program is loaded. The loading of UNIX is essentially the same whether it is initially loaded from a floppy disk or a hard drive. The bootstrap program is always located at a specific physical disk address. Generally, the bootstrap program will be found on disk device 0, track 0, cylinder 0 and block 0. The hardware is responsible for locating and loading the bootstrap program.

When the bootstrap begins execution it searches a special stand-alone directory (/stand) for the stand-alone shell program (sash). The sash program is loaded and begins execution. From this stand-alone shell, the UNIX operating system can be loaded, or other stand-alone programs such as fsck (the file system check program) may be executed. The UNIX operating system is loaded and executed from the stand-alone shell.

Once the loading of UNIX has begun, the following general sequence of events occurs. The CPU is initialized along with memory. The system control programs init, sched and xsched are loaded and executed. The general startup program /etc/rc is executed and each terminal is activated with /etc/getty, /bin/login, and after login, /bin/sh.

STARTUP AND INITIALIZATION

The first step in loading UNIX is the execution of a program called start. The start program initializes the CPU which includes determining the amount of memory available and clearing that memory. It then loads and executes the modules called mlsetup( ) and main( ). In the course of this execution, the processes init(always process id 1) and xsched are created.

The mlsetup( ) routine performs several functions critical to the start of UNIX execution. The system page table entries for text, data, user block and stack are allocated. The memory bit map is initialized. This begins as process 0, and the process table is initialized for this process. Finally, the various machine registers are assigned.

After mlsetup( ) completes its execution, the main( ) routine is executed. This routine invokes msginit( ) to initialize the system message queues and seminit( ) to initialize the system semaphore map. The process newproc( ) is invoked to create the init( ) system process.

When newproc( ) runs to create init( ), it first calls expand( ) to get address space for the init( ) process. Once the space is allocated, the copyout( ) process copies instructions from the kernel text to the newly allocated address. These instructions are the code to cause the execution of /etc/init in the allocated init address space.

Once init( ) has been started, newproc( ) is again executed to create the swapper process xsched( ) which will have process I.D. 2. Finally, sched( ) is called to start the swapper routine.

During the course of the startup, several processes are invoked to initialize the system tables. Figure 14-1 describes the system table initialization processes.

/etc/init. The /etc/init process is the ancestor of all processes except processes 0 and 1. It creates and ultimately kills all processes. This process

Process	Function
inainit()	Link inode entries into ifreelist
clkstart()	Start system clock
cinit()	Link clists into cfreelist
binit()	Link buffer headers into bfreelist, empty hash lists
errinit()	Initialize error map
finit()	Link file table entries into ffreelist
iinit()	Initialize root file system information
vpminit()	Initialize virtual protocol information
x25init()	Initialize x25 driver
stinit()	Initialize synchronous terminal driver

Fig. 14-1. System table initialization processes.

is controlled by data in the /etc/inittab table. It maintains its own table of information containing data about the state of each of the processes it has or will spawn.

The /etc/init process is signal driven. Most of its time is spent waiting for a signal and when it receives an appropriate signal it checks /etc/inittab and its own process table to determine the status of the process for which it received a signal.

The /etc/inittab table contains a set of instructions about which process or processes to spawn depending on the current system state. The table consists of a set of records containing a process identifier, a process state identifier, an action, and a program specification. The fields in the table are separated by colons. When /etc/init reads the table, if the current state matches the state in a table record, it will execute the program specification as shown in Fig. 14-2.

Two very important tasks are spawned by /etc/init in the course of starting UNIX. First, the /etc/rc process is executed. This process starts all processes that are important while the system is running. It is a user-modifiable process and so can be used to start user processes. Typically, /etc/rc mounts the file systems, starts any background daemons (processes that run in the background), cleans up the system by removing any residual temporary files and starts the system accounting processes.

The second process spawned by /etc/init is /etc/getty. The getty process sets the terminal information for each terminal on the system and then invokes /bin/login so that a user can logon at a terminal. This process is run for each terminal on the system. It is table-driven from the file /etc/gettydefs. The /etc/gettydefs file contains the parameters necessary for starting each terminal.

Once the /etc/getty process is complete, it executes the /bin/login process for each terminal. The login process accepts a password and checks /etc/passwd for a matching password. If a password is found, the user environment corresponding to that password in the /etc/passwd file is established. Finally, the user shell is executed and the user is able to use the UNIX operating system.

SYSTEM TERMINATION

System termination is initiated by the system administrator logged on as the superuser. The termination is initiated when the command /etc/shutdown is entered at the shell prompt.

The first task of /etc/shutdown is to perform the sync( ) call. The sync( ) call ensures that all system inodes, buffers and superblocks have been flushed to the disk. Next a warning message is sent to all users indicating that system shutdown will occur in a specified period of time. The shutdown process then

```
rc::wait:/etc/rc 1 /dev/console 21
co::respawn:/etc/getty console console
23:2:respawn:/etc/getty -t60 tty23 2400
```

Fig. 14-2. Sample /etc/inittab entries.

149

sleeps until the time period has elapsed. Once shutdown has been awakened, accounting is turned off, remote job entry is terminated, error recording is stopped, and all other processes are terminated. Any mountable file systems are dismounted and the system is switched to single user mode. Finally, another sync( ) is performed.

System accounting is turned off with the command /usr/lib/acct/shutacct. This process appends terminating records to the accounting files and kills the accounting processes.

The /etc/errstop command kills the error processing. Error recording is performed by the/ err/demon process and is stopped by a signal sent from the /etc/errstop process.

All remaining processes are killed with the /etc/killall process. Once the system is in single user mode, it can be safely powered off and UNIX operation terminated.

OF INTEREST TO PROGRAMMERS

The most programmable feature of all the UNIX initiation and termination processes is the /etc/rc process. This is entirely user-modifiable and should be freely used to modify the runtime environment of the UNIX system. In addition it is possible to modify the /etc/inittab and /etc/gettydefs tables. Modification of these tables will result in different terminal and system runtime environments.

Note that error recording and system accounting can be discontinued at any time with no ill-effect on system performance. These processes should be used or not used at the discretion of the system administrator depending on the intended use of the UNIX operating system. They will probably be of little value when the UNIX system is being used as a single-department development machine, but will be of considerably more value when the system is being used by several departments or in production.

Summary

Starting and stopping the UNIX operating system is much like any other operating system. The main event which must occur is the location, loading and initiation of the bootstrap program. This bootstrap program is usually located at a specific, physical disk location.

The bootstrap program for UNIX causes the loading and execution of the standalone shell. Once the standalone shell has determined that the system is ready, it causes the invocation of the start program. The start program initializes the CPU. Once the CPU has been initialized, init is loaded and executed. init becomes the ancestor of all processes.

Three processes execute at UNIX initiation time. The /etc/rc process is the basic start up process—it mounts file systems, cleans up the system and generally performs the housekeeping duties. The terminal characteristics are loaded and terminals made ready for use by the /etc/getty process. Finally, /bin/login sets the login procedures for each of the terminals.

Shutting down the UNIX system is straightforward. The /etc/shutdown command causes the issuance of the sync( ) call followed by kill signals being sent to all processes. Once all the processes are dead, the system shifts to single user mode where it can be entirely shut down and powered off.

Points to Ponder

What is the reason for first loading the stand alone shell? Why not simply begin initiation of the main UNIX system?

Miscellaneous UNIX Facilities

The UNIX operating environment provides two sets of facilities which while optional, can provide important information to system administrators. They are accounting and error reporting. The system accounting functions provide data regarding process and user performance and usage. The error reporting facility helps track system errors and make system maintenance and error correction easier.

SYSTEM ACCOUNTING

All of the system accounting functions rely on UNIX's ability to keep track of time and relative time intervals. UNIX maintains a time identifier. The time identifier is a long integer which contains the number of seconds since 00:00:00 Greenwich Mean Time on January 1, 1970. When the UNIX system is booted the time identifier is set to the value contained in s_time member of the root file system super block by the iinit( ) function. The time identifier is used whenever absolute time is needed.

The *time of day register* (TODR) is the hardware time of day clock register. This register maintains the number of 10-millisecond clicks since 00:00:00 Greenwich Mean Time on January 1 of the current year. If for any reason the TODR register is not updated every 10 milliseconds (for example, if the battery backup should fail), it will contain a 0. This register is used to reset the system time (the time identifier) after a power failure.

Finally, the lbolt identifier contains the number of clock ticks since the system was last booted. This value is used to determine relative times to a high degree of accuracy.

Three types of accounting are provided by UNIX: process accounting, connect time accounting and disk usage accounting.

Process accounting tracks user mode time and system mode time for each process. The data for this accounting is recorded in the file /usr/adm/pacct file. The data is recorded in this file by the kernel every time a process terminates. In addition to the time, process memory usage is also recorded. In Fig. 15-1, process accounting data in the user block is illustrated.

The data fields are updated every clock interrupt. User mode times or system mode times are updated depending on the current process mode. The clock routine also recomputes the u_mem field if the process is currently running. The memory size for a process at any time is the sum of its data size plus its textsize divided by the number of active processes sharing the text. The accounting data is recorded to the accounting file when the process terminates.

Figure 15-2 shows the fields recorded in the process accounting record of the accounting file.

Four commands are used to control process accounting. The acctcom command prints the process accounting files. The commands acctprc1 and acctprc2 when used in combination print the per user process accounting data both by the user and in the summary. The command summary and usage is obtained with acctcms. Finally, the turnacct command turns system accounting on and off.

```
User Block                      Contents

Accounting field


u_utime                         Process user mode time

u_stime                         Process system mode time

u_cutime                        Descendent process user mode time

u_cstime                        Descendent process system mode time

u_tsize                         Process current text in clicks

u_dsize                         Process current data size in clicks

u_mem                           Accumulated memory usage in clicks
```

Fig. 15-1. Process accounting data in user block.

Field	Contents	Derivation
ac_flag	Accounting Flag	u_acflag
	--No execution	
	--Used super user privileges	
	--Normal	
ac_stat	Exit status	exit_status
ac_uid	Accounting user I.D.	u_ruid
ac_gid	Accounting group I.D.	u_rgid
ac_tty	Controlling terminal	u_ttyd
ac_btime	Beginning time	u_start
ac_utime	User mode time	u_utime
ac_stime	System mode time	u_stime
ac_etime	Elapsed time	lbolt-u_ticks
ac_mem	Memory usage	u_mem
ac_io	Characters transferred	u_ioch
ac_rw	Blocks read or written	u_ior+u_iow
ac_comm	Command name	u_comm

Fig. 15-2. Accounting record fields.

Connect time accounting tracks the length of a user's terminal session from logon to logoff. The file /etc/utmp contains a record of the current status of each port while /etc/wtmp contains a cumulative history of each status change for each port. The init( ) process creates and initializes /etc/utmp and /etc/wtmp. Note that init( ) does not create /etc/wtmp if it does not exist.

The command /usr/lib/acct/acctcon1 prepares a report in which a series of records of logon/logoff activity is reported as a sequence of records, one per login session, and reports the associated connect time. Summary accounting records are produced from the aoutput of acctcon1 by /usr/lib/acct/acctcon2. The commands /etc/fwtmp and /etc/wtmpfix are used to modify connect time accounting files.

Disk usage accounting is reported by the /usr/lib/acct/acctdusg command. The output from this command is used to produce summary accounting records by the /usr/lib/acct/acctdisk command.

SYSTEM ERRORS

There are three error categories on the UNIX system: hardware errors, software errors and events causing the panic function. While these three categories are not always entirely distinct, it is useful to consider error in this way.

Hardware (device) errors can be reported as one of three types of error. A block device error is a read, write or similar type of I/O error. A stray interrupt is an error resulting because an interrupt was detected at an unexpected time. Memory parity errors indicate some type of memory failure. When one of these errors is detected, it is reported by the device driver by the functions logberr( ) (for block errors), logstray( ) (for stray interrupt errors), and logmemory( ) (for memory parity errors).

The reported errors are stored in one of seven record types. One type of error record is the error logging startup record. Error logging termination is the second type of record. System time and configuration each compose distinct error record types. Finally, block device, stray interrupt and memory parity each have their own record type. The error records are placed in linked lists with the type of record having its own linked list.

The errors can be retrieved by reading from a special device called /dev/error. This device is a software character device. The driver of the /dev/error device provides the functions erropen, errclose and errread. For system users this is a read only device.

The program /usr/lib/errdaemon is the system error logging function. It reads errors from the /dev/error device and writes them in the /usr/adm/errfile. The error logging daemon can only be started by the superuser (usually it is started in /etc/rc) and only one daemon can be running at a time. There are five types of system software errors. These errors are listed in Fig. 15-3.

When a system error occurs the appropriate member of the kernel data structure (syserr) is incremented. The syserr structure resides in the kernel data space at all times. It is allocated at system configuration time. The structure has one count field for each of the five types of the system software errors.

Errors which do not fit one of the categories already described are not resolvable by the kernel. When the kernel detects one of these situations, it invokes the panic function. Fatal or unresolvable situations occur if no file system is found, or a bad memory map is located for example. When the panic function is invoked a warning message is printed at the system console and all system activities are suspended.

```
Inode table overflow

File table overflow

Text table overflow

Process table overflow

Synchronous Backplane Interface (SBI) errors
```

Fig. 15-3. System software errors.

OF INTEREST TO PROGRAMMERS

The accounting functions can be used to tune system performance. All programmers responsible for system performance should spend some time analyzing the various accounting reports to determine if the various processes are making efficient use of memory, disk and swapping resources.

It is also important to occasionally analyze the error reports. High numbers of unexplained device or software errors may provide some advance warning of system failure.

Summary

UNIX provides two facilities for helping to measure and improve system performance. The system accounting functions allow data storage and reporting on memory usage, connect time, CPU usage and disk usage. Several facilities are provided to produce formatted reports on this data. System errors also provide useful system information. Stored in the file /dev/error, the data on system errors reflects the status of hardware errors, software errors and system panics (unresolvable kernel errors).

Points to Ponder

What is the best way to use the system accounting facilities so that their execution does not affect system performance?

What types of events would cause system panics?

Appendices

Appendix A:
UNIX V System Calls

The following is a list of all the UNIX System V system calls. Note that unless otherwise specified a system call returns 0 if it is successful and − 1 when an error occurs. This list gives only a brief description of these calls. For full detail please consult either the *UNIX System V Programmer Reference Manual* or the *UNIX System V Interface Definition*.

```
/* abort—generate an abnormal process abort */
int        abort( )

/* access—determine file accessibility */
char       *path;                          /*  path naming file
                                               */
int        amode;                          /*  mode of access:
                                                   04
                                               read
                                                   02
                                               write
                                                   01
                                               execute
                                                   00
                                               existence */

int        access(path, amode)
```

```
/* acct—enable or disable process accounting */
char        *path;                              /* path name of
                                                   accounting file */


int         acct(path)

/* alarm—set process alarm clock */
unsigned sec;                                   /*   seconds till alarm
                                                     */

unsigned alarm(sec)

/* chdir—change working directory */
char        *path;                              /*   path name  of
                                                     directory */

int         chdir(path)

/* chmod—change mode of file */
char        *path;                              /*   path naming file
                                                     */
int         mode;                               /*   access mode:
                                                         04000
                                                     Set user ID on
                                                     execution
                                                         02000
                                                     Set group ID on
                                                     execution
                                                         01000
                                                     Save text image
                                                     after execution
                                                         00400
                                                     Read by owner
                                                         00200
                                                     Write by owner
                                                         00100
                                                     Execute      by
                                                     owner
                                                         00040
                                                     Read by group
                                                         00020
                                                     Write by group
                                                         00010
                                                     Execute by group
                                                         00004
                                                     Read by others
                                                         00002
                                                     Write by others
                                                         00001
```

```
int       chmod(path, mode)
```

/* chown—change file owner and group */

```
char      *path;                              /*  path naming file
                                                 */
int       owner,                              /*  owner I.D. */
          group;                              /*  group I.D. */
int       chown(path, owner, group)
```

/* chroot—change root directory */
```
char      *path;                              /*  path of new
                                                 directory */

int       chroot(path)
```

/* close—close a file descriptor */
```
int       fildes;                             /*  file descriptor */
int       close(fildes)
```

/* creat—create a new file */
```
char      *path;                              /*  path naming file
                                                 */
int       mode;                               /*  open mode (same
                                                 as chmod) */

int       creat(path, mode)
```

/* dup—duplicate an open file descriptor */
```
int       fildes;                             /*  file descriptor */
int       dup(fildes)                         /*  returns file
                                                 descriptor */
```

/* exec—takes the form execl, execv, execle, execlp, execvp all forms execute
a file */
```
char      *path,                              /*  path naming file
                                                 */

          *file,                              /*  file name */
          *arg0,                              /*  passed argument
                                                 */

.
.
.

          *arg1,                              /*  passed argument
                                                 */

          *argn,                              /*  passed argument
                                                 */
```

```
              *argv[ ],                               /*  list of arguments
                                                          */
              *envp[ ];                               /*  environment */
int           execl(path, arg0, arg1, . . ., argn, (char *)0)
int           execv(path,argv)
int           execle(path,arg0, arg1, . . ., argn, (char *)0, envp)
int           execve(path, argv, envp)
int           execlp(file, arg0, arg1, . . ., argn, (char *)0)
int           execvp(file, argv)

/* exit—terminate a process (also exit) */
int           status;                                 /*  termination
                                                          status */

void          exit(status)
void          exit(status)
/* fclose—close or flush a stream (also fflush) */
#include stdio.h
FILE          *stream;                                /*  stream pointer */
int           fclose(stream)
int           fflush(stream)


/* fcntl—file control */
#include fcntl.h
int           fildes,                                 /*  file descriptor */
              cmd;                                    /*  command */
int           fcntl(fildes, cmd, arg)                 /*  arg is specific to
                                                          command */


/* ferror—stream status inquiries */
#include stdio.h
FILE          *stream;                                /*  stream pointer */
int           ferror(stream)
int           feof(stream)
void          clearerr(stream)
int           fileno(stream)

/* fopen—open a stream (also freopen, fdopen) */
#include stdio.h
char          *file-name,                             /*  file name */
              *type;                                  /*  type of open:
                                                                "r" open
                                                          for reading
                                                                "w"
                                                          truncate or create
                                                          for writing
                                                                "a"
                                                          append; open for
```

```
                                                        writing at end of
                                                        file, or create for
                                                        writing
                                                                "r + "
                                                        open for update
                                                                "w + "
                                                        truncate or create
                                                        for update
                                                                "a + "
                                                        append */
FILE        *stream;                            /*   stream pointer */
int         fildes;                             /*   file descriptor */
FILE        *fopen(file-name, type)
FILE        *freopen(file-name, type, stream)
FILE        *fdopen(fildes, type)

/* fork—create a new process */
int         fork( )

/* fread—binary read/write (also fwrite) */

#include stdio.h
char        *ptr;                               /*   array pointer */
int         size,                               /*   number of bytes
                                                     of I/O */

            nitems;                             /*   number of items
                                                     */
FILE        *stream;                            /*   stream pointer */
int         fread(ptr, size, nitems, stream)
int         fwrite(ptr, size, nitems, stream)
/* fseek—reposition a file pointer (also rewind, ftell) */
#include stdio.h
FILE        *stream;                            /*   stream pointer */
long        offset;                             /*   position offset */
int         ptrname;                            /*   current position:
                                                         0
                                                     beginning of file
                                                             1 current
                                                     position
                                                             2 end of
                                                     file */

int         fseek(stream, offset, ptrname)
void        rewind(stream)
long        ftell(stream)

/* getcwd—get current working directory */
```

```
char        *buf;                                    /*  buffer for path
                                                         name */
int         size;                                    /*  buffer length */
char        *getcwd(buf, size)


/* getpid—get process, process group and parent process ids */
int         getpid( )                                /*  process I.D. */
int         getgrp( )                                /*  group I.D. */
int         getppid( )                               /*  parent I.D. */


/* getuid—get real user, effective user, real group, effective group */
unsigned short getuid( ) /* user I.D. */
unsigned short geteuid( ) /* effective user I.D. */
unsigned short getgid( ) /* group I.D. */
unsigned short getegid( ) /* effective group I.D. */


/* ioctl—control device */
int         fildes,                                  /*  file descriptor */
            request;                                 /*  function to be
                                                         performed */
int         ioctl(fildes, request, arg)              /*  arg is request
                                                         specific */


/* kill—send a signal to a group of processes */

int         pid,                                     /*  process I.D. */
            sig;                                     /*  signal to send */
int         kill(pid, sig)


/* link—link to a file */
char        *path1,                                  /*  path name of
                                                         existing file */

            *path2;                                  /*  path name of new
                                                         file */

int         link(path1, path2)


/* lockf—record locking on files */
int         fildes,                                  /*  file descriptor */
            function;                                /*  control value */
long        size;                                    /*  number of bytes
                                                         locked/unlocked
                                                         */

int         lockf(fildes, function, size)


/* lseek—move read/write file pointer */
int         fildes;                                  /*  file descriptor */
```

```
long        offset;                                 /*  offset of seek */
int         whence;                                 /*  starting  position
                                                        */

long        lseek(fildes, offset, whence)


/* malloc—main memory allocator (also free, realloc, calloc, mallopt, mallinfo)
*/
#include malloc.h
unsigned    size;                                   /*  bytes to
                                                        allocate */

char        *ptr;                                   /*  memory
                                                        location */

unsigned    nelem,                                  /*  number of
                                                        elements */

            elsize;                                 /*  element size
                                                        */

int         cmd,                                    /*  command */
            value;                                  /*  control value
                                                        */

char        *malloc(size)                           /*  returns
                                                        pointer  to
                                                        memory */

void        free(ptr)
char        *realloc(ptr, size)
char        *calloc(nelem, elsize)
int         mallopt(cmd, value)
struct      mallinfo mallinfo( );


/* mknod—make a directory or special/ordinary file */
char        *path;                                  /*  new file path */
int         mode,                                   /*  mode of new file
                                                        */

            dev;                                    /*  device of new file
                                                        */

int         mknod(path, mode, dev)


/* mount—mount a file system */
char        *spec,                                  /*  block file system
                                                        to be mounted */

            *dir;                                   /*  mounted on
                                                        directory */

int         rwflag;                                 /*  write permissions
                                                        */

int         mount(spec, dir, rwflag)


/* msgctl—message control operations */
```

```
#include sys/types.h
#include sys/ipc.h
#include sys/msg.h
int          msqid,                                    /*  message  queue
                                                           identifier */

             cmd;                                      /*  control operation
                                                           */

struct       msqid_ds *buf;                            /*  data for operation
                                                           */

int          msgctl(msqid, cmd, buf)

/* msgget—get message queue */
#include sys/types.h
#include sys/ipc.h
#include sys/msg.h
key_t        key;                                      /*  message  queue
                                                           identifier */

int          msgflg;                                   /*  message flag */
int          msgget(key, msgflg)

/* msgop—message operations */
#include sys/types.h
#include sys/ipc.h
#include sys/msg.h
int          msqid;                                    /*  queue  identifier
                                                           */

struct       msgbuf *msgp;                             /*  structure
                                                           containing
                                                           messages */

int          msgsz;                                    /*  length of text */
long         msgtyp;                                   /*  type  of message
                                                           */

int          msgflg;                                   /*  action to be taken
                                                           */

int          msgsnd(msqid, msgp, msgsz, msgflg)
int          msgrcv(msqid, msgp, msgsz, msgtyp, msgflg)

/* nice—change priority of a process */
int          incr;                                     /*  increment to nice
                                                           value */

int          nice(incr)

/* open-open for reading/writing */
#include fcntl.h
char         *path;                                    /*  path naming file
                                                           */
```

```
int        oflag,                                      /*  open type flag */
           mode;                                       /*  open mode */
int        open(path, oflag [, mode])
```

/* pause—suspend process until signal */
```
int        pause( );
```

/* pipe—create an interprocess channel */
```
int        fildes[2];                                  /*  file descriptors
                                                           for read and
                                                           write pipes */

int        pipe(fildes)
```

/* plock—lock process, text, or data in memory */
```
int        op;                                         /*  lock type */
int        plock(op)
```

/* popen—initiate pipe to/from a process (also pclose) */
```
#include stdio.h
char       *command,                                   /*  command line
                                                           pointer */

           *type;                                      /*  pipe type */
FILE       *stream;                                    /*  stream pointer */
FILE       *popen(command, type)
int        pclose(stream)
```

/* profil—execution time profile */
```
char       *buff;                                      /*  area in memory
                                                           to contain data */

int        bufsiz,                                     /*  length of buffer
                                                           */

           offset,                                     /*  offset from user
                                                           program counter
                                                           */

           scale;                                      /*  multiplication
                                                           factor */

void       profil(buff, bufsiz, offset, scale)
```

/* ptrace—process trace */
```
int        request,                                    /*  trace action */
           pid,                                         /*  process I.D. */
           addr,                                        /*  address location
                                                           being traced */

           data;                                       /*  data being traced
                                                           */

int        ptrace(request, pid, addr, data)
```

```
/* read—read from a file */
int          fildes;                                /*  file descriptor */
char         *buf;                                  /*  buffer to read
                                                        into */

unsigned  nbyte;                                    /*  bytes to read */
int          read(fildes, buf, nbyte)

/* semctl—semaphore control operations */
#include sys/types.h
#include sys/ipc.h
#include sys/sem.h
int          semid,                                 /*  semaphore  I.D.
                                                        */

             cmd;                                   /*  command */
int          semnum;                                /*  semaphore
                                                        number */

union        semun arg;                             /*  semaphore  data
                                                        area */

int          semctl(semid, semnum, cmd, arg)

/* semget—get a set of semaphores */
#include sys/types.h
#include sys/ipc.h
#include sys/sem.h
key_t      key;                                     /*  semaphore key */
int          nsems,                                 /*  number of
                                                        semaphores */

             semflg;                                /*  semaphore flag */
int          semget(key, nsems, semflg)

/* semop—semaphore operations */
#include sys/types.h
#include sys/ipc.h
#include sys/sem.h
int          semid;                                 /*  semaphore  I.D.
                                                        */

struct       sembuf **sop;                          /*  semaphore
                                                        operations */

int          nsops;                                 /*  number  of
                                                        semaphore
                                                        operations */

int          semop(semid, sops, nsops)

/* setpgrp—set process group I.D. */
int          setpgrp( )
```

```
/* setuid—set user and group I.D.s (also setgid) */
int        uid;                                    /*  user I.D. */
int        gid;                                    /*  group I.D. */
int        setuid(uid)
int        setgid(gid)

/* shmctl—shared memory control operations */
#include sys/types.h
#include sys/ipc.h
#include sys/shm.h
int        shmid,                                  /*  shared  memory
                                                       I.D. */

           cmd;                                    /*  shared  memory
                                                       command */
struct     shmid__ds *buf;                         /*  shared  memory
                                                       buffer */


int        shmctl(shmid,cmd,buf)

/* shmget—get shared memory segment */

#include sys/types.h
#include sys/ipc.h
#include sys/shm.h

key__t     key;                                    /*  shared  memory
                                                       key */
int        size,                                   /*  memory size */
           shmflg;                                 /*  activity flag */
int        shmget(key, size, shmflg)

/* shmop—shared memory operations (see text) */

/* sleep—suspend execution for interval */
unsigned   seconds;                                /*  length of
                                                       suspension */

unsigned sleep(seconds)

/* stat—get file status (also fstat) */
#include sys/types.h
#include sys/stat.h
char       *path;                                  /*  path naming file
                                                       */
struct     stat *buf;                              /*  status buffer */
int        fildes;                                 /*  file descriptor */
```

```
int        stat(path, buf)
int        fstat(fildes, buf)


/* stime—set time */
long       *tp;                                    /* seconds since
                                                      00:00:00  GMT,
                                                      Jan 1, 1970 */

int        stime(tp)


/* sync—update superblock */
void       sync( )

/* system—issue a command */
#include stdio.h
char       *string;                                /*  command string
                                                       */

int        system(string)


/* time—get time */
long       *tloc;                                  /*  location to store
                                                       returned time */

long       time(tloc)
long       time((long *)0)


/* times—get process and child process elapsed times */
#include sys/types.h
#include sys/times.h
struct     tms *buffer;                            /*  time data buffer
                                                       */

long       times(buffer)


/* ulimit—get and set user limits */
int        cmd;                                    /*  command */
long       newlimit;                               /*  file size limit */
long       ulimit(cmd, newlimit)


/* umask—set and get file creation mask */
int        cmask;                                  /*  file  mode
                                                       creation mask */

int        umask(cmask)


/* umount—unmount a file system */
char       *spec;                                  /*  pointer  to  path
                                                       name */

int        umount(spec)
```

```
/* uname—get name of current UNIX system */
#include sys/utsname.h
struct     utsname *name;                              /*  name data buffer
                                                           */

int        uname(name)

/* unlink—remove directory entry */
char       *path;                                      /*  path naming file
                                                           */

int        unlink(path)

/* ustat—get file system statistics */
#include sys/types.h
#include ustat.h
int        dev;                                        /*  device   number
                                                           containing
                                                           mounted    file
                                                           system */
struct     ustat *buf;                                 /*  status buffer */
int        ustat(dev, buf)

/* utime—set file access and modification times */
#include sys/types.h
char       *path;                                      /*  path naming file
                                                           */

struct     utimbuf *times;                             /*  time buffer */
int        utime(path, times)

/* wait—wait for child process to stop or terminate */
int        *stat_loc;                                  /*  process   status
                                                           location */

int        wait(stat_loc)
int        wait((int *)0)

/* write—write on a file */
int        fildes;                                     /*  file descriptor */
char       *buf;                                       /*  buffer to write */
unsigned   nbyte;                                      /*  number of bytes
                                                           to write */

int        write(fildes, buf, nbyte)
```

Appendix B: UNIX Signals

Value	Type	Description
01	SIGHUP	hangup
02	SIGINT	interrupt
03	SIGQUIT	quit
04	SIGILL	illegal instruction
05	SIGTRAP	trace trap
06	SIGIOT	IOT instruction
07	SIGEMT	EMT instruction
08	SIGFPT	floating point exception
09	SIGKILL	kill
10	SIGBUS	bus error

11	SIGSEGV	segmentation violation
12	SIGSYS	bas argument to system call
13	SIGPIPE	write on pipe with no one to read it
14	SIGALRM	alarm clock
15	SIGTERM	software termination
16	SIGUSR1	user defined signal 1
17	SIGUSR2	user defined signal 2
18	SIGCLD	death of a child
19	SIGPWR	power failure

Appendix C:
Shell Command Summary

The chart below provides a list of all the basic shell commands available in UNIX and XENIX, presented in alphabetical order by command.

The brief descriptions provided are not intended to substitute for the detailed documentation to be found in the UNIX and XENIX reference manuals. Instead, they are intended to provide a brief reminder of the capabilities available.

The columns for UNIX V and XENIX V indicate whether these commands and system calls are available in only one or both systems.

Command	UNIX V	XENIX V	Description
300	•		handle DASI 300 and 300s terminals
4014	•		handle pagination on Tektronix 4014 terminal
450	•		handle DASI 450 special features
acctcom	•	•	print process accounting file
accton		•	turns on accounting
accept		•	accept print requests
admin	•	•	create and administer SCCS files
ar	•	•	archive maintainer
arcv	•		convert PDP-11 archives to standard
as	•	•	Assembler
asa	•		handle ASA printer characters
asktime		•	get correct time of day
assign		•	assign devices
at	•	•	execute commands at a later time
awk	•	•	string scanning and processing
backup		•	perform incremental file backup
banner	•	•	create posters
basename	•	•	get parts of path names
bc	•	•	calculator
bdiff	•	•	file comparison
bfs	•	•	big file scanning
bs	•		small program compiler
cal	•	•	print calendar
calendar	•	•	daily reminder
cat	•	•	concatenate
cb	•	•	C program beautifier
cc	•	•	C compiler
cd	•	•	change working directory

Command	UNIX V	XENIX V	Description
cdc	•	•	change delta comment for SCCS
cflow	•		generate flow diagram of C program
chgrp		•	change group i.d.
chmod	•	•	change file mode
chown	•	•	change file owner
chroot		•	change root i.d. for command
clockrate		•	set interrupt timer clock frequency
clri		•	clear inode
cmp	•	•	compare files
col	•	•	filter reverse line feeds
comb	•	•	combine SCCS deltas
comm	•	•	select or reject common lines between two files
convert	•		change archive formats to common forms
copy		•	copy groups of files
cp	•	•	copy files
cpio	•	•	copy file archives
cpp	•	•	C preprocessor
cprs	•		compress IS25 object file
crontab	•		display user crontab file
crypt	•	•	encrypt/decrypt file
csplit	•	•	split line on context
ct	•	•	spawn getty to remote process
ctrace	•		C program debugger
cu	•	•	call a different UNIX system
custom		•	customize XENIX V
cut	•	•	cut selected fields
cxref	•		C program cross reference
date	•	•	get/set date

Command	UNIX V	XENIX V	Description
dc	•	•	desk calculator
dd	•	•	convert and copy file
delta	•	•	create delta to SCCS file
devnm		•	identify device name
df		•	reports free disk blocks
diff	•	•	file comparison
diff3	•	•	three-way file comparison
diffmk	•	•	mark differences between files
dircmp	•	•	compare directories
dirname		•	get part of path name
dis	•		disassembler
disable		•	turn off terminals
diskcp		•	copy/compare floppy disks
divvy		•	divide disk partitions
dmesg		•	display system messages on console
doscat		•	display DOS file
doscp		•	copy files between XENIX and DOS
dosdir		•	display DOS directory (DOS format)
dosls		•	display DOS directory (UNIX format)
dosmkdir		•	create DOS directory
dosrm		•	delete DOS file
dosrmdir		•	remove DOS directory
dtype		•	determine disk type
du	•	•	disk usage summary
dump	•	•	dump selected portions of object files
dumpdir		•	print name of files on backup archive
echo	•	•	repeat arguments
ed	•	•	text editor
edit	•		text editor
efl	•		extended Fortran language

Command	UNIX V	XENIX V	Description
enable	•	•	enable/disable line printers
env	•	•	set shell environment
ex	•	•	text editor
expr	•	•	evaluate arguments
f77	•		Fortran 77 compiler
factor	•	•	factor a number
file	•	•	determine file type
find	•	•	locate files
finger		•	display user information
fixhdr		•	change binary file header
format		•	format floppy disk
fsck	•	•	check and repair file system
fsplit	•		split Fortran files
gdev	•		graphic routines
ged	•		graphic editor
get	•	•	get an SCCS file
getopt	•	•	parse command options
graph	•		draw a graph
graphics	•		access graphics commands
greek	•		select terminal filter
grep	•	•	search file for pattern
grpcheck		•	check group file
gutil	•		graphic utilities
haltsys		•	close file system and halt cpu
hd		•	display files in hexadecimal
head		•	print beginning of stream
help	•	•	ask for help
hp	•		handle Hewlett-Packard 2640 and 2621 terminals

Command	UNIX V	XENIX V	Description
hpio	•		handle Hewlett-Packard 2645A tape archiver
hyphen	•		locate hyphenated words
id	•	•	print user and group i.d.'s
ipcrm	•	•	remove message queue, semaphore set or shared memory i.d.
ipcs	•	•	report interprocess communications status
ips		•	IMAGEN serial sequence packet protocol handler
join	•	•	relational database operator
kill	•	•	terminate a process
l		•	list directory contents
lc		•	list directory contents in columns
ld	•	•	link editor
lex	•	•	lexical analysis program generator
line	•	•	read one line
lint	•	•	C program analyzer
list	•		produce C source from object files
ln	•	•	link to a file
login	•	•	sign on
logname	•	•	get login name
lp	•	•	control requests to line printer
lpadmin		•	configure line printer
lpstat	•	•	display line printer status
ls	•	•	list directory contents
m4	•	•	macro processor
machid	•		provide information about processor type
mail	•	•	send or read mail
make	•	•	automatic program maintainer

Command	UNIX V	XENIX V	Description
makekey	•	•	generate encryption key
man	•	•	print manual entries
mesg	•	•	permit or deny messages to terminal
mkdir	•	•	create directory
mkfs	•	•	construct file system
mknod	•	•	build special file
mkuser	•	•	add login i.d. to system
more		•	view file one screen at a time
mount	•	•	mount a file system
mv	•	•	rename file or directory
ncheck		•	get names from inode numbers
netutil		•	administer XENIX network
newform	•		change text file format
newgrp	•	•	log in to new group
news	•	•	print news
nice	•	•	set nice value
nl	•	•	number lines
nm	•	•	print name list of common object
nohup	•	•	prevent termination due to hangup
od	•	•	octal dump
pack	•	•	expand and compress files
passwd	•	•	change password
paste	•	•	merge file lines
pg	•	•	screen-at-a-time file viewing filter
pr	•	•	print files
prof	•	•	display profile data
ps	•	•	print SCCS file
pstat		•	report system information
ptx	•	•	create permuted index

Command	UNIX V	XENIX V	Description
pwadmin		•	perform password aging administration
pwcheck		•	check password file
pwd	•	•	print working directory
quot		•	summarize file system ownership
random		•	generate random number
ratfor	•		rational Fortran language
rcp		•	copy files across XENIX systems
red	•	•	restricted **ed**
regcmp	•	•	regular expression compiler
remote		•	execute commands on remote XENIX system
rjestat	•		RJE status report
rm	•	•	remove files or directories
rmdel	•	•	remove delta for SCCS
rmuser		•	remove user from system
rsh	•	•	restricted shell
runbig		•	run commands too large for memory
sact	•	•	print current SCCS file status
sag	•		system activity graph
sar	•		system activity reporter
sccsdiff	•	•	SCCS file comparison
sdb	•		symbolic debugger
sddate		•	set backup date
sdiff	•	•	file comparison
sed	•	•	stream editor
send	•		submit RJE jobs
setcolor		•	set screen color
setmmt	•	•	establishes /etc/mnttab table
settime		•	change access and modification times of files

Command	UNIX V	XENIX V	Description
sh	•	•	invoke shell
shl	•		shell layer manager
shutdown	•	•	terminate all processing
size	•	•	report object size
sleep	•	•	suspend execution temporarily
sno	•		SNOBOL interpreter
sort	•	•	sort file
spell	•	•	spell check file
spline	•	•	interpolate smooth curve
split	•	•	split file into pieces
stat	•		statistical network
strip	•	•	strip symbol and line number information from object
stty	•	•	set terminal characteristics
su	•	•	become super user or different user
sum	•	•	print files checksum and block count
sync	•	•	update the superblock
sysadmin		•	perform file system backups and restores
tabs	•	•	set terminal tabs
tail	•	•	get last part of file
tar	•	•	tape archiver
tee	•	•	pipe fitting
test	•	•	evaluate command condition
time	•	•	time a command
timex	•		time a command
toc	•		graphic table of contents
touch	•	•	update access and modification times for a file
tplot	•		graphics filters

Command	UNIX V	XENIX V	Description
tput	•		query **terminfo** database
tr	•	•	translate characters
true	•	•	provide truth values
tsort	•	•	topological sort
tty	•	•	get terminal name
umask	•	•	set file creation mode mask
un53ctl	•		set USART communications interface registers
uname	•	•	print current system name
unget	•	•	undo a previous SCCS **get**
uniq	•	•	report repeated lines
units	•	•	conversion
uuclean	•	•	clean up **uucp** spool directory
uucp	•	•	UNIX to UNIX communications
uustat	•	•	**uucp** statistics
uuto	•	•	UNIX to UNIX file copy
uux	•	•	UNIX to UNIX command execution
val	•	•	validate SCCS file
vc	•		version control
vi	•	•	full screen text editor
wait	•	•	await process completion
wc	•	•	word count
what	•	•	identify SCCS files
who	•	•	who is on the system
whodo		•	who is doing what
write	•	•	write to another user
xargs	•	•	construct argument list and execute command
yacc	•	•	yet another compiler compiler
yes		•	print string repeatedly

Appendix D: ATT System V Versus BSD UNIX

One of the ways in which Bell Laboratories began to popularize the UNIX operating system was to distribute at very low cost (or in some cases free) to colleges and universities. In providing a base of UNIX trained users, this distribution into an environment of experimentation led to a number of enhancements of the UNIX operating system.

The University of California at Berkley was one of the major universities to receive UNIX. The modifications and enhancements made to the UNIX at Berkley were so great that soon they had their own distribution and following. The Berkley System Distribution (BSD) UNIX now has its own group of loyalists and a sufficient following in the UNIX community to be creating a certain amount of controversy over which UNIX should be the standard or "real" UNIX. The rest of this appendix will briefly highlight the major features of BSD UNIX as they differ from ATT UNIX.

The first feature of BSD UNIX which is now incorporated in a modified form into ATT UNIX is job control. Job control allows the user to work on several tasks simultaneously, switching between them (in a sense activating them) as required. With job control foreground tasks can be placed in the background and background tasks retrieved and made foreground tasks.

Electronic mail is available in some form in all UNIX implementations, but BSD UNIX provides a sophisticated mailx command. The mailx command is a greatly enhanced mail command. The mailx command allows an editor such as vi to be used to edit electronic mail during composition. It summarizes all the waiting messages when invoked. It automatically keeps a copy of the mail you send. It allows you to create group aliases for sending mail to large groups. Finally, it allows customization for individual needs.

The vi full screen editor is now available in almost all UNIX implementations, but it was born and developed at Berkeley.

Those familiar with the ATT UNIX environment are also probably familiar with the Bourne shell interface. BSD UNIX features the C shell—with features targeting programmers. The key features of the C shell are: its ability to evaluate expressions; its array processing capabilities; its file overwrite and accidental logoff protection; its command history; its command aliasing mechanism; its auto-execution capabilities; and its use of control structures to control execution within a shell script. The C shell is now available in most UNIX environments, even non-BSD UNIX systems.

The fsck (file system utility consistency check) developed at Berkeley is the same as the standard fsck in most respects. It incorporates a -p option which causes fsck to ask questions only if a repair would be destructive.

The more filter is a part of BSD UNIX. It allows you view a file a screen at a time. It allows automatic editor invocation and single line or half screen program scrolling. The pg command in the ATT UNIX environment emulates portions of this utility.

The Berkeley implementation allows 4-8K disk blocks for data storage versus the 1K block used in ATT UNIX. Since this could result in considerable wasted space, BSD UNIX allows for block fragments to store the file ending fragments of several files.

BSD UNIX has modified signal handling somewhat. It has an additional system call which allows a process to block and unblock the receipt of signals. The kernel does not send a signal to a process that has blocked that signal until the process unblocks for that signal. Thus, signals are not lost on processes unable or unready to receive them. They are held by the kernel until the process is ready. In addition, receipt of a signal can mean the interruption and stoppage of a system call in progress. The BSD kernel has the ability to automatically restart the system call once signal processing is complete.

Demand paging, the swapping of portions of the process image instead of the entire process image, was first implemented in BSD UNIX. It is now available in ATT System V.

The fork( ) system call makes physical copies of the parent process image. If an exec( ) call is to follow immediately, the physical copying is an unnecessary use of system resources, since the process image will immediately be overlaid with the new process image. BSD UNIX provides a vfork( ) call which assumes that the exec( ) call is going to follow immediately and only prepares the memory location, but does not physically copy the parent process image.

All UNIX I/O is interrupt driven. It is at times convenient to be able to poll devices however. BSD UNIX provides a select( ) system call that allows device polling.

One of the major additions made by BSD UNIX which is important in today's environment where connectivity is a critical issue is the inclusion of the socket mechanism. Sockets provide a common method for interprocess communication while allowing the use of network protocols. A kernel structure consisting of a socket layer, a protocol layer and device driver layer is created. This structure allows the processes to plug into the socket without regard for the protocol. This mechanism provides a more generalized framework for network support.

These are the major differences between ATT UNIX and BSD UNIX. BSD has provided some valuable enhancements, but it is less widely used than ATT UNIX. It is likely that the BSD will continue to be incorporated into ATT UNIX over time.

Appendix E: UNIX In a Multiprocessor Environment

UNIX was of course designed to run in a single CPU, single processor environment. The multiprocessor environment consists of several CPU's sharing common memory and peripherals. The hoped for gain in the multiprocessor environment is greater throughput since more processes can run concurrently. From the user view, UNIX in a multiprocessor environment should be a perfect fit—as processes are spawned, they get their own processors allowing true simultaneity instead of time sliced concurrency. Unfortunately, it is not that easy.

The critical problem with UNIX in a multiprocessor environment is that kernel and process data corruption can occur quite easily. Two processes running simultaneously on different processors using the same data structures could easily both try to read or write at the same time. This is clearly a problem. There are two straightforward solutions to dealing with multiprocessor UNIX environments.

One effective implementation of a solution is to define a master and slave processor relationship. In this arrangement, one processor, defined as the master handles all the kernel processing (including scheduling). The other processors run only the user mode processing. In this way, the master processor can control the simultaneous use of memory structures through judicious scheduling. The drawback to this approach is that throughput is not what it could be in a multiprocessor environment. There will be kernel processing bottlenecks as the load on the system increases.

The other working solution is to use a sophisticated set of semaphores and locks. Each process and processor is responsible for locking and protecting critical regions of memory as those regions are used. Thus, the processes run as fast as they can, waiting only for critical shared memory to be freed. In this approach, throughput is maximized. The drawback here is that sloppy programming can neglect to use the proper locking and freeing techniques and still cause corruption to occur.

It is possible to have effective UNIX implementations in a multiprocessor environment. Several companies are doing so. Some UNIX kernel modifications are necessary to make UNIX a truly efficient multiprocessor operating system.

Glossary

abort( )—system call to generate an abnormal process abort.

access( )—system call to determine accessibility of a file.

acct( )—system call to enable or disable system accounting.

address space—locations for data in the user area.

alarm( )—system call to set a process alarm clock.

algorithms—problem solving techniques.

a.out—default output for the successful compilation of a C program.

alloc—routine to allocate additional core memory.

allocated inode list—kernel list of inodes in use.

auxiliary swapper—also called xsched, handles voluntary swap outs.

/bin/login—the login process invoked following /etc/getty.

base priority—the non-changing initial priority of a process.

baud rate—data transmission speed in bits per second.

bit—the smallest unit of information.

bit flag—a flag which consists of exactly one bit.

block addresses—physical disk addresses of data blocks.

boot block—disk block which contains the bootstrap program.

booted system—initialized UNIX system.

bootstrap program—program which contains instructions for loading UNIX.

breada—block read algorithm.

breadf—block read algorithm.

brelse—block release algorithm.

buffers—segments of storage in main or secondary memory.

bwrite—block write algorithm.

C—primary programming language in the UNIX environment.

canonical I/O—also known as cooked, terminal I/O with special processing completed.

cc—UNIX C compiler.

character buffers—low speed, non-reusable memory buffer.

character devices—devices which process a character at a time.

child directories—directories which are the offspring of a parent.

chdir( )—system call to change the current directory.

chmod( )—system call to change file permissions.

chown( )—system call to change file ownership.

chroot( )—system call to change the effective root.

clist—character list used with terminal I/O.

close( )—system call to close an open file.

click—the smallest unit of memory.

completion interrupt—signal sent to indicate end of I/O.

context of a process—swapping image of a process.

core—main memory.

coremap—memory map of main memory.

CPU—controlling processor.

creat( )—system call to create a new file.

cron—clock timer process.

Ctrl-d—end of file character in UNIX.

/dev/error—file containing recorded system errors for hardware,software and panics.

daemons—background processes.

death of a child—signal indicating termination of a child process.

default action—action to be taken when a signal is received.

demand paging—memory management technique in which portions of processes are swapped instead of entire process images.

device drivers—software modules controlling data between processes and devices.

device files—special files representing physical devices.

device interrupts—signals indicating I/O status.

device numbers—numbers indicating driver and port for device.

devices—I/O hardware.

direct block pointers—addresses of file data blocks on disk.

directories—files containing files and inumbers.

direct memory access—memory access directly from device, nonbuffered.

dirty buffers—memory buffers which have been used and not updated to disk.

DMA—direct memory address.

dup( )—system call to duplicate a file handle.

erase characters—terminal I/O characters which delete the preceding character.

events—system occurrences which trigger other system occurrences.

exec( )—system call to execute a file.

executable files—a file which contains instructions for loading and running.

exit( )—system call to terminate a process.

fclose( )—system call to close or flush a stream.

fcntl( )—system call for file control.

ferror( )—system call for stream status inquiries.

FIFO—first in, first out.

194

file descriptors—numbers used to refer to open files.
file path name—parents needed to access file from the root.
file system—UNIX organization of files.
file system check—fsck utility program to check consistency of file system.
file types—either directory, named pipe, regular or special.
fopen( )—system call to open a stream.
fork( )—system call to create a new process.
fread( )—system call for binary input/output.
fsck —see file system check.
fseek( )—system call to reposition a file pointer in a stream.

getcwd( )—system call to get the path name of the current working directory.
getpid( )— system call to get the process id.
getuid( )—system call to get the user id.

hashing algorithm—technique for locating data based on its content.
heap—memory space allocated during a programs runtime.
hierarchical file systems—tree structured file systems.

ignore action—instruction to ignore signal sent.
indirect block pointers—addresses of blocks containing disk block addresses.
init( )—ancestor to all UNIX processes except 0 and 1.
initialization—UNIX boot.
inode—data structure containing administrative data about a process.
inode numbers—numbers referencing inodes.
inode reference count—number of times inode is currently being accessed.
interprocess communication—transfer of data or information between processes.
interrupts—hardware signals of device activity.
ioctl( )—system call to control device.

kernel—the true operating system portion of UNIX.
kernel address space—main memory used by the kernel.
kernel mode—process operating mode in high priority.
kill( )—system call to send a signal.

LIFO—last in, first out.
line discipline modules—modules which interact with terminal device drivers.
link( )—system call to link to a file.
locked inode—inode currently in exclusive use by another process.
lockf( )—system call to do record locking.
lseek( )—system call to move the read/write file pointer.

magic numbers—operating system assigned numbers with special meaning.
main( )—driving module of a C program.
malloc( )—system call to allocate memory.
messages—interprocess communication facility for sending unformatted data.
mkfs—system administrator utility to create a file system.
mknod( )—system call to make a file.
mount( )—system call to mount a file system.
mount—to logically attach a new file system to an existing one.

mount table—table containing information on mounted file system.
msgctl( )—system call for message control operations.
msgget( )—system call to get a message queue.
msgop( )—system call for message operations.

named pipes—interprocess communication facility using FIFO files.
namei( )—algorithm for deriving a file name from an i-number.
nice( )—system call to change process priority.
nice value—user adjustable process priority setting.

open( )—system call to open a file.
orrery—planetary motion simulation.

page—segment of memory.
panic function—non-resolvable kernel error.
path—list of directories from root to final destination.
pause( )—system call to suspend a process until a signal.
permissions—user, group and others privileges with respect to a file.
pipe( )—system call to create an interprocess channel.
pipes—named or unnamed, FIFO files.
popen( )—system call to initiate a pipe to and from a process.
primary memory—core or main memory.
processes—running programs.
process context—system environment during process execution.
process I.D.—number identifying a process.
process image—the non-running memory picture of a process.
process preemption—non-voluntary process stopping because the time quantum has
  elapsed.
process switching—changing of the running process.
process synchronization—coordination of data sharing between concurrently
  executing processes.
process tracing—interprocess communication facility used primarily in debugging.
profil( )—system call to produce execution time profile.
ptrace( )—system call for a process trace.

quantum—UNIX unit of time measurement.

read( )—system call to read from a file.
Ritchie, Dennis—co-author of UNIX and C.
root directory—ancestor of all other directories.
run queue—processes waiting and available to be run.

sash—stand alone shell.
sbrk( )—routine to free allocated memory.
sched( )—routine to handle the swapping in of processes to main memory.
scheduling algorithm—technique for determining which process to execute.
sdb—symbolic debugger.
semaphores—interprocess communication facility using multiple flags.
semctl( )—system call for semaphore control.
semget( )—system call to get a set of semaphores.
semop( )—system call to perform semaphore operations.

setgrp( )—system call to set group id.

setuid( )—system call to set user id.

shared memory—interprocess communication facility using common memory between two or more processes.

shared-text processes—processes sharing common code segments.

shell—user interface to UNIX operating system.

shmctl( )—system call for shared memory control operations.

shmget( )—system call to get a shared memory segment.

shmop( )—system call to perform shared memory operations.

sleep( )—system call to suspend execution for some interval.

stack—data space used for passed parameters.

stat( )—system call to get file status.

stime( )—system call to set time.

superblock—data block containing status of file system.

superuser—user with full set of permissions.

swap device—secondary memory storage device.

swapping image—that portion of a process image required for execution.

sync( )—system call to update the superblock.

system( )—system call to issue a command.

system calls—calls requesting kernel functions on behalf of user process.

termio.h—include file containing terminal characteristics.

text segment—code portion of process image.

Thompson, Ken—author of UNIX.

time( )—system call to get time.

times( )—system call to get process and child process elapsed times.

time sharing operating system—UNIX, for example.

ulimit( )—system call to get and set user limits.

umask( )—system call to set and get file creation mask.

umount( )—system call to unmount a file system.

uname( )—system call to get name of current UNIX system.

UNIX—multiuser, multiprocessing time sharing operating system.

unlink( )—system call to remove a directory link.

user area—memory dedicated to user process execution.

ustat( )—system call to get file system statistics.

utime( )—system call to set file access and modification times.

wait( )—system call to wait for child process to stop or terminate.

write( )—system call to write to a file.

x25driver—device driver for x.25 communications protocol.

zombie process—process still in process table but with no swapping image.

Bibliography

AT&T Bell Laboratories. *UNIX System V Interface Definition, Issue 1.* Short Hills, N.J.: AT&T, 1985.

Bach, Maurice J. *The Design Of The UNIX Operating System.* New Jersey: Prentice-Hall Inc. 1986.

Banahan, Mark, and Rutter, Andy. *The UNIX Book.* New York: John Wiley and Sons, 1983.

Bourne, S.R. *The UNIX System.* Reading, Mass.: Addison-Wesley, 1982.

Christian, Kaare. *The UNIX Operating System.* New York: John Wiley and Sons, 1983.

Clukey, Lee Paul. *UNIX And XENIX Demystified.* Blue Ridge Summit, Pa.: TAB BOOKS Inc., 1985.

Comer, Douglas. *Operating System Design: The XINU Approach.* New Jersey: Prentice-Hall, Inc. 1984.

Feuer, Alan. *C Puzzle Book.* Englewood Cliffs, N.J.: Prentice-Hall, 1982.

Gauthier, Richard. *Using The UNIX System.* Englewood Cliffs, N.J.: Reston Publishing Company Inc., 1981.

Gehani, Narain. *Advanced C: Food For The Educated Palate.* Potomac, Md.: Computer Science Press, 1985.

Guthery, Scott B. *Learning C with tiny-c.* Blue Ridge Summit, Pa.: TAB BOOKS Inc., 1985.

Kernighan, Brian, and Pike, Rob. *The UNIX Programming Environment.* Englewood Cliffs, N.J.: Prentice-Hall, 1984.

- - - - - -, and Ritchie, Dennis. *The C Programming Language.* Englewood Cliffs, N.J.: Prentice-Hall, 1978.

Lomuto, Ann and Nico. *A UNIX Primer.* Englewood Cliffs, N.J.: Prentice-Hall, 1983.

McGilton, Henry, and Morgan, Rachel. *Introduction to the UNIX System.* New York: McGraw-Hill, 1983.

Osterhaug, Anita. *Guide To Parallel Programming.* Beaverton, Oregon: Sequent Computer Systems, Inc. 1985.

Plum, Thomas. *C Programming Standards and Guidelines.* Cardiff, N.J.: Plum Hall Inc., 1982.

- - - - - -*Learning to Program in C.* Cardiff, N.J.: Plum Hall Inc., 1983.

Rochkind, M.J. "The Source Code Control System." *IEEE Transactions on Software Engineering,* December 1975.

Shaw, Myril C. and Shaw, Susan S. *UNIX V And Xenix System V Programmer's Tool Kit.* Blue Ridge Summit, Pa.: TAB BOOKS, Inc. 1986.

Sobell, Mark G. *A Practical Guide To UNIX System V.* Memlo Park, CA.: The Benjamin/Cummings Publishing Company, Inc. 1985.

Thomas, Rebecca, and Yates, Jean. *User Guide to the UNIX System: Includes Berkeley and Bell System V.* Berkeley, Calif.: Osborne/McGraw-Hill, 1983.

UNIX System V Documents. Greensboro, N.C.: Western Electric Co., 1985.

"UNIX Time-Sharing System." *The Bell System Technical Journal,* July-August, 1978.

Waite, Mitchell; Prata, Stephen; and Martin, Donald. *C Primer Plus.* Indianapolis: Howard W. Sams and Co., 1984.

Zahn, C.T. *C Notes.* New York: Yourdon Press, 1983.

Index

Index

Edited by David Gauthier

Other Bestsellers From TAB

☐ **80386—A PROGRAMMING AND DESIGN HANDBOOK—Penn Brumm and Don Brumm**

The basis of IBM's much-anticipated OS/2 operating system and their new Personal System/2 computers, the 80386 microprocessor promises new standards in microcomputer power, speed, and versatility. Now, with the cooperation of 80386 designers from Intel Corporation, Penn and Don Brumm have provided the first complete sourcebook on this advanced processor, including an overview of its capabilities and in-depth information for programmers and designers. 448 pp., 150 illus.

Paper **$19.95**   Hard **$29.95**
Book No. 2937

☐ **CLIPPER™: dBASE® COMPILER APPLICATIONS—Gary Beam**

Whether you are a novice Clipper user in need of hands-on guidance in mastering the compiler's many special functions and features or an experienced program developer looking for new techniques to enhance your programming efficiency, this book is a must. And, to save you the time and effort of typing the programs and routines included by Beam, there is a set of two ready-to-run disks available that include both application program code and interactive utilities. 190 pp., 37 illus.

Paper **$16.95**   Book No. 2917

☐ **POWER PROGRAMMING WITH ADA® FOR THE IBM PC®—John Winters, Ph.D.**

This excellent new guide puts Ada programming within easy understanding. Whether you'd simply like to find out how Ada works or you need a fundamental knowledge of Ada to compete more effectively in the Defense Department-related marketplace, John Winters leads you easily and effectively through the principles of Ada programming from step one to actual program writing. He even includes an extensive glossary filled with sample code that's an ideal programming reference. 220 pp., 153 illus.

Paper **$16.95**   Hard **$24.95**
Book No. 2902

☐ **WORKING WITH FOCUS®: AN INTRODUCTION TO DATABASE MANAGEMENT—Clifford A. Schaffer**

Every aspect of this powerful, business-oriented software system is covered . . . from building and entering a database, the parts of FOCUS, and the format of data fields to entering data, FOCUS reports, the text editor, the Dialogue Manager, and user-n language. With the help of this comprehensive reference, you'll be able to develop applications more than twice as fast under FOCUS than general-purpose languages. 256 pp., 91 illus.

Paper **$22.95**   Book No. 2810

☐ **INTRODUCTION TO TELECOMMUNICATIONS SYSTEMS—P. H. Smale**

This sourcebook covers the whole range of telecommunication principles, beginning with a basic discussion of wave theory and continuing with the principles behind radio, television, telephone, and digital networks. Covers all the latest technology in telecommunications: local area networks (LANs), cellular phones, cable television, direct broadcasting by satellite, high-definition television, optic fiber systems, and mobile radio systems. 160 pp., 181 illus.

Paper **$14.95**   Book No. 2924

☐ **WORKING WITH ORACLE®—Jack L. Hursch, Ph.D., and Carolyn J. Hursch, Ph.D.**

This easy-to-understand guide shows you how you can use the ORACLE database management system to open the lines of communication between all the computers in your company—micros, minis, and mainframes. The ideal supplement to the ORACLE user's manual, this book addresses all the standard operations and features of ORACLE version 5.0. with instructions on ORACLE's query language, SQL. 240 pp., 75 illus.

Paper **$19.95**   Book No. 2916

☐ **SYSTEMS DESIGN UNDER CICS COMMAND AND VSAM—Alex Varsegi**

Here is a comprehensive summary of CICS functions, design considerations, and related software products to acquaint you with the concept of on-line data processing and its established role in current computer design. You'll cover system design, screen painting techniques using SDF to create input/output maps, the use of CECI, VSAM (virtual storage access method), all the CICS commands and how they relate to system design. 272 pp., 204 illus., 6″ × 9″.

Hard **$28.95**   Book No. 2843

☐ **Smart Apples: 31 ARTIFICIAL INTELLIGENCE EXPERIMENTS WITH THE APPLE II®, II + ®, IIe®, IIc®, and IIGS®—Delton T. Horn**

This unique book will help you enter the world of AI using only an Apple computer. The treasury of programs can turn your computer into an intelligent competitor, a witty conversationalist, an artist, poet, musician, or writer. Horn includes an introduction to intelligence research and covers the milestones in AI development. You'll cover such intriguing topics as the Turning Test, game applications, computer-generated stories, and more. 200 pp., 47 illus.

Paper **$12.95**   Hard **$18.95**
Book No. 2775

Other Bestsellers From TAB